'DEAREST MOTHER'

The Letters of F. R. Kendall

EDITED BY
Brian MacDonald

|L|L|P|

Lloyd's of London Press Ltd
Legal Publishing and Conferences Division
One Singer Street
London, EC2A 4LQ

USA AND CANADA
Lloyd's of London Press Inc
Suite 523, 611 Broadway
New York, NY 10012, USA

GERMANY
Lloyd's of London Press
59 Ehrenbergstrasse
2000 Hamburg 50
West Germany

SOUTH EAST ASIA
Lloyd's of London Press (Far East) Ltd
903 Chung Nam Building
1 Lockhart Road, Wanchai
Hong Kong

ISBN 1-85044-220-7

Cover Design, Artform
Text set in 10pt Times by Cristina Kennedy and Brian MacDonald
Printed in Great Britain by
Billings and Sons Ltd., Worcester

They that go down to the sea in ships,
that do business in great waters;
These see the works of the Lord,
and his wonders in the deep

FOR THE MISSIONS TO SEAMEN
AND THOSE THEY SERVE

Foreword

BY H.R.H. PRINCESS ANNE, THE PRINCESS ROYAL
PRESIDENT, THE MISSIONS TO SEAMEN

As President of The Missions to Seamen I am delighted to be able to pay tribute to the generosity of Mr. Brian MacDonald and to his parent company, P&O. All the royalties from this book will be paid by the publishers to The Missions.

It is only when we look back at personal records such as these letters that we appreciate fully how much has changed since the middle of the last century, and how much stays constant.

The Missions to Seamen was founded in the year that Franklin Richardson Kendall joined P&O, to follow in his father's footsteps. It remains with us today, still carrying out the same sterling work on behalf of seamen around the world. Seamen are, as ever, the backbone of the shipping industry and in spite of the changes, The Missions to Seamen is still needed and they need your support. Thank you.

October 1988

v

Taken in
London
around 1858.

Taken in
Melbourne
around 1866.

1 Franklin Richardson Kendall

Contents

Illustrations

Introduction

When I joined P&O in 1961, I was privileged to work in its London Head Office at 122 Leadenhall Street.

As someone interested in history, I was able to explore vast store-rooms containing letters and files dating back to the company's origins in the 1840's. Here was history which one could reach out and touch: letters to the Pasha about the building of the Suez Canal, intelligence reports from overseas offices giving updates on situations in China, India and other parts of the world. There were voyage reports from ships' Captains; in the main these reported on cargoes taken up and discharged or on the passengers being carried but, now and again, on some local situation such as, for example, how the Indian Mutiny was affecting local trading conditions.

At the end of 1963, '122' was demolished to make way for a modern office block. Although many papers were removed and sent to the National Maritime Museum at Greenwich, of necessity, many were either destroyed or left in one of the building's sub-basements to be later built upon. In those last few months, I took the opportunity of browsing through some of the papers which were to be left.

One evening, I came across a volume of letters written by a P&O Assistant, F. R. Kendall, to his mother between 1858 and 1866. There were seventy-eight letters, each commencing with the words "My Dearest Mother", describing his various travels over three hundred pages.

The volume remained substantially unread for some years until, doing research for an article I was then writing, I examined them in detail. Kendall's was an exciting time in which significant world-wide social and industrial changes were being made, and I read, with mounting interest, his comments on the state of upheaval which existed in the Empire and of troubles simmering in Europe, the Far East and America.

I am glad to have the opportunity of presenting here a selection of extracts from Kendall's letters and hope you also will share in his sense of adventure and enjoy his pithy comments on all that was going on around him.

About the Writer

Franklin Richardson Kendall was born on 2 December 1839 into a Cornish family with a history reaching back into the Crusades. More recently, his family had strong naval traditions: Great-Grandfather was

1

Admiral Thomas Hicks (*"who had the honour of being ... known to his late Majesty William IV"*) and Grandfather, Edward Kendall, a Captain. The family also had strong Church connections.

His father, Lt. Edward Nicholas Kendall, had a distinguished naval career. He served with distinction on several Arctic expeditions, including one under Sir John Franklin, and on a number of scientific and survey voyages. Possibly on account of failing health, he retired from the Navy in 1840 and joined the West India Mail Company, moving to P&O shortly afterwards as Superintendent of their Southampton base. He marked his connection with exploration by bestowing his eldest son with the names of two explorers, Richardson and Franklin; the latter appears to have been a relation.

Unfortunately, we know very little of Kendall's mother. There were four children; Mary who married and who died in Calcutta in 1858, Franklin, Edward who became a clergyman in England and Sinclair who followed his brother into the P&O service.

Educated at Christ's Hospital, Kendall joined P&O on 1 January, 1856 at a salary of £30. He was sent to Bombay in 1858 as an Assistant and later served in Singapore, Hong Kong, Calcutta, Bombay and Melbourne. He returned to London in 1881, living in Blackheath, and retired on a pension of £1,000 in 1906, having reached the position of Chief General Manager. He died on 23 December, 1907.

Kendall's marriage in 1867 produced six sons and a daughter. Nicholas became a doctor, Franklin an architect, Edward a businessman, Charles an Indian High Court Judge, Frederick joined the Hong Kong and Shanghai Bank and Herbert followed his father into P&O. All the sons, except Nicholas, spent considerable parts of their careers abroad. Mary, with three brothers on either side of her, died aged twenty six.

The sons, like their father, were prodigious letter writers and regularly corresponded with each other for many years by means of 'Round Robins' and each added to a notebook his own news and comments and passed it on. One hundred and sixty five quarto-sized notebooks of these Round Robins, covering the period 1903 to 1945, are now in the custody of the Royal Institution of Cornwall in Truro and will be available for publication in the year 2000.

Kendall was writing in the heyday of Victorian Britain and the Raj, and his comments reflect the attitudes of that time. To Kendall, the 'white man's burden' was predominantly an English one, and while he could be critical of the 'natives' he encountered and appeared to think so little of, he rises quickly, for example, to the defence of the Vietnamese who, he thought, were abused by the French colonialists to an extent which would not be tolerated by the British. Aged nineteen when he left Britain to go out East, his views are essentially those of a middle-class English colonialist whose life was regulated by the arrival and departure of 'the mail' and whose social calendar was governed by status and position in society. Kendall was no exception and he ensured that he called on the right people and attended the correct functions.

His style of writing is uncomplicated, although many of his comments could be acid, doubtless since they were meant for a limited circulation which may also explain the occasional names which one suspects were dropped in from time to time for effect. Nevertheless, he comes over as an intelligent, inquiring and enthusiastic man of many abilities, not the least of which was his ability to walk prodigious distances on his various strolls ashore.

In selecting the extracts included in this book, I have omitted much material which is purely personal as well as that which is repetitive. Where dates are available, I have included them, but since Kendall would start a letter, lay it aside and add to it later, the date on which a particular section of a letter may have been written is not always apparent.

About P&O

Brodie McGhie Willcox, a London shipbroker, and an ex-Royal Navy clerk, Arthur Anderson, built up a shipping business linking Britain with the Iberian peninsula in the 1820's and 30's, and began regular steamer sailings with the *William Fawcett* in 1835.

P&O, as it later became, laid its foundations on government contracts to carry mails by steamship. Formal incorporation as The Peninsular & Oriental Steam Navigation Company did not come until 1840, but before P&O was very old it had already considered 1837, the year of its first mail contract, to be its true foundation.

The founders put their own money and ships into the business, but they needed mail contracts to give it financial stability, while the Royal Charter granted in 1840 enabled them to raise the £1 million of capital, far beyond their own resources, for the eastward expansion that they envisaged.

In 1840 P&O opened a service to Egypt and three years later extended eastwards to India. The two sections were linked by the celebrated "Overland Route" across the land barrier between the Mediterranean and the Red Sea. Covering 150 miles, it used canal boats from Alexandria to the Nile, a small river steamer up to Cairo and horse-drawn coaches across the desert to Suez, though a railway was built later.

By 1845, P&O steamers reached Singapore and Hong Kong and its routes were extended to Sydney in 1852 and Japan in 1859. When the French completed the Suez Canal in 1869, P&O found itself with an unsuitable fleet and falling revenue.

It recovered under the leadership of Thomas (later Sir Thomas) Sutherland. He overhauled its operations and ensured that the size, speed and standards of its vessels remained pre-eminent east of Suez. The mail routes to India, the Far East and Australia remained P&O's main preoccupation. Renewed contracts required ever quicker and sometimes more frequent deliveries and the quantity of mails steadily increased.

So too did the number of passengers; two-thirds of those bound for India were on government service, but there were also bankers, planters, industrialists, European and Indian princes, world travellers, cricket teams, and the young ladies known as the "Fishing Fleet" who were looking for husbands.

The company's full history is told in The Story of P&O by David Howarth and Stephen Howarth, published by Weidenfeld & Nicolson.

My research of Kendall and the incidents he mentions took place primarily between 1966 and 1968 when a full edition of his letters was produced internally for P&O. At that time, I had invaluable assistance from representatives of P&O, The India Office, The National Maritime Museum, The Times and many other organisations including overseas offices and agents of P&O as well as surviving members of the Kendall family. Since then, I have moved my offices on a number of occasions with the result that the original research correspondence has been lost.

While this prevents me from thanking specific individuals for their ready assistance, I am nevertheless grateful and indebted for their help.

I am also grateful to Times Newspapers Ltd. for permision to use the extract from the Times on page 16, to The Illustrated London News Picture Library for permission to use the prints on pages 56, 96, 138, 148, 155 and 170 and to P&O in respect of the remaining material.

August 1988   Brian MacDonald

1
On Board "Ripon"

February 17th, 1858

My Dearest Mother,
We are a great deal more fortunate than I expected in arriving at Gibraltar. The old *Ripon* has done wonders, having made one of the quickest, if not the quickest, runs she has ever made from Southampton to Gibraltar.[1] We were alongside the coalhulk at Gibraltar yesterday afternoon at half past two, just under five days from Southampton.[2]

We there found the *Alhambra* waiting with steam up, and the Blue Peter flying to take the mail for England, so that we just caught her nicely. I did not expect we should have caught her at Gibraltar as she ought to have started the day before, but she was a day behind her time in consequence of having met with a gale of wind nearly the whole way out! She left Southampton on the eighth, calling at Vigo, Oporto, Lisbon and Cadiz en route.

Our average speed from Southampton has been about 230 nautical miles a day, or nearly ten knots an hour the whole distance, Gibraltar being 1151 nautical miles from Southampton.

The view of Gibraltar from the sea is charming, and the approach to it for miles is most beautiful. We passed close to the little town of Tarifa about noon. It is a small town, beautifully situated on the coast at the foot of mountains, which are partly wooded nearly the whole way down, and altogether the scenery was most charming. As the ship was steaming into the bay, we had a good view of the fortifications, Dockyard, etc., guns peeping out of all sorts of impossible places at a tremendous height, and houses dotted about here and there on the sides of the hills. It reminded one altogether more of some giant's castle in a fairy tale than a real orthodox fortification. There were a good many ships and a steamer or two going in and out, and a larger ship sailing in nearly held her own with us though we were going fully ten knots.

In order to prevent our being cheated by the boatmen, the stewards issued boat tickets at 1/- each to go on shore, and accordingly a party of about eight embarked on board one of the boats alongside (of course directly she was alongside the hulk, boats swarmed round the ship). We landed and signed our names in a book, and then I went with two of the passengers to take a stroll in the principal street.

I don't know any English town that Gibraltar is the least like. I think that it reminded me more of Plymouth than any other place I have been in though, of course, it is very different to that. The numbers of people in the streets of all nations, apparently, under the sun, were marvellous, Moors whose only dress was a sort of loose robe hanging down over their loins, with a turban or fez on their head and Morocco slippers on their feet, Spaniards, Portuguese, French, English, Egyptian, etc., etc., at every corner. The houses are high in the principal streets, but the windows are small and covered with a sort of close-fitting venetian shutter.

The jargon of people jabbering to one another is fearful, and it is most amusing to see a row between two or more men. We saw several. If any of them had been English, he would have his coat off and shirt sleeves up, and pommelling away in no time, but they only shove one another and talk loud and quick and swear, looking all the time as though their eyes were coming out of their heads.

It was the last day of the carnival at Gibraltar and everybody is allowed to dress up as they like and parade the streets. Lots of children were marching about, decked in all sorts of gay costumes, and there were several men dressed as women, and women as men. One man made such a capital woman, that it if had not been for his awkward way of walking, and his great clumsy feet one would not have known that he was not one. I think I saw one or two of the prettiest and some of the ugliest women I ever saw.

I should like to have bought something, but was afraid to go into a shop for fear of having my eyes cheated out of my head. There were lots of men and boys in the streets selling baskets of oranges containing three or four dozen splendid fellows for 6d. Several of the passengers bought baskets of them and have been scrambling them this morning among the soldiers. It was most amusing to see how some of these longheaded Scotch fellows (and indeed others as well) got taken in. One man had invested in three or four pounds of tobacco at 7/6d a pound, which he thought he had got a great bargain, but found afterwards that he might have got the same for 4/6d or 5/- a pound at home. Another man bought a very ordinary straw hat for 4/6d which blew overboard, and nearly everyone who was green at it got taken in somehow or other.

After I came on board, I went to see Mr. Paine's brother, the Captain of the coalhulk.[3] He is a funny old fellow, rather like his brother in face, but in everything else as unlike him as chalk to cheese. He is a most eccentric individual, and though he has been at Gibraltar I think about twelve or thirteen years, they say he has only once been on shore. There are curious stories told of him, in fact nearly all the officers in the service have some story to tell of "old Paine". They say he was shipwrecked on a desert island, and only one man with him, and that one night the other man put out the light before he wanted him to, and that after that they never spoke to one another though they were six months alone in the island.

February 19th

We left Gibraltar at eight o'clock on Tuesday evening, and on Wednesday were well into the Mediterranean. It was rather wet in the morning, which called forth an observation that it was rather curious that the first day we got into the Mediterranean we should have "made it-a-rainy-'un". I felt rather seedy, not sea-sick, on Wednesday and no better yesterday, principally caused, I think, by my taking a glass of beer at tiffin on Wednesday, which I had not done before since I came on board.[4] I made an attack last night upon the compound rhubarb pills, which I hope will set me all right again.[5] There is no lack of doctors on board, as there are three (all Scotch) passengers, besides the ship's doctor. We did not have service on board on Wednesday (Ash Wednesday) but we had salt fish at dinner.

The motion of the ship yesterday was far from pleasant as, though we were to all appearances in a calm, there was a heavy swell, which made the ship pitch and roll, and do both together in fine style. Today we have a head wind and a high confused sea, topmasts struck and gaffs lowered, but I do not think the motion is worse than yesterday.[6] They say if we were in a fast screw we should be all pitched out of our beds almost in weather like this, but the old *Ripon* keeps steadily on, like an easy-going craft she is.

Everything is done on board in regular man-of-war style. The ropes are all coiled as neatly as possible, the yards well squared, (except when going head to wind) and the bells sounded punctually every half hour, the decks are well scrubbed every morning, and everything is as clean and neat as can be. When we were going into Gibraltar the little *Alhambra* was lying at anchor and flying a pennant, as the Admiralty Agent was on board.[7] One of the passengers, a sailor, was looking at her and asked what war steamer that was. "Oh," said I, "that is the *Alhambra*, she only flies the pennant because there is a Lieut. in the navy on board". "Nonsense", said he, "you never see a merchant steamer's rigging in such order as that." Really, speaking without prejudice, if you see a P&O steamer alongside any other

7

merchant steamer, I don't care what service, you will see the difference directly.[8]

I never saw troops so comfortably berthed in my life as they are on board the *Ripon*.[9] They have plenty of room, and everything they have is clean and comfortable. In many cases the owners of a steamer of the *Ripon's* size would have had 700 or 800 men at least on board, besides the first class passengers and officers, but we have only 235. I do not suppose we shall any of us be so comfortable on the other side, as there will be a good many passengers from Marseilles, and the *Madras* is not nearly so large as the *Ripon*. [10]

If we had continued to have the same weather as hitherto, I think we should have been at Malta tomorrow night but, as it is, we shall not be there till some time on Sunday. I only hope that the *Teviot* won't beat us, but I don't think she will, as we made so good way to Gibraltar. I hear that the Superintendent of the West India Mail Co. has threatened to have the ship laid up if she is not at Alexandria as soon as we are. She does not call at Gibraltar, so she will have a slight advantage over us in the actual running distance, besides avoiding detention there, but I expect she will have to stay at Malta longer than we shall as she will have more coal to take on board.[11]

7 p.m. It has been blowing a gale of wind ahead this afternoon, the sea very rough, and the ship's figurehead frequently taking a bath, but still we have shipped hardly any water, though as one or two of us were looking over the bows just after dinner to see how she took it, we got drenched to the skin by one wave, which seemed to take a peculiar fancy for us, and gave as good practical proof that the Mediterranean is not a freshwater sea. I think since dinner today I have felt less squeamish than almost any other day I have been on board. I have not been sick since the day in the Bay of Biscay, and hope I may not be but I expect when we get into a fast screw on the other side, we shall get the benefit.

The ducks on board signify their disapprobation by quacking as loud as they can every time the ship pitches. The fowls give proof of seasickness by being more and more attenuated every day when they come to table. The geese have a curious trick of putting their heads to the wall, and their backs to the front of the cages, which provokes mischievously inclined individuals to give a tug at their tails as they pass. The sheep I think appear to be as well as any of the livestock.[12] The little pony is lively. He gets a trot round the ship every day and seems very well now, but he was very ill the first day or two.

The ladies are all in their cabins today. One was venturesome enough to try to come out at dinner time, but had to retire precipitately. Several of the gentlemen too are laid up.

February 20th

I must say my romantic ideas of the Mediterranean are rather dispelled. I had fancied it rather a sort of fairy sea, the water so clear that one might almost see the bottom, and the sky so perfectly clear and cloudless, whereas instead of a clear blue sky we have had one very nearly approximating the colour of slate, and the blue water ditto except when one looks over the bows and sees them cut through the water, when it certainly is a beautiful dark blue.

I have not yet donned my thin trousers, etc., as I have not been at all uncomfortably warm in the others, but I find it rather necessary to alter my diet. I take no meat at breakfast, only a little fish or a couple of eggs or something else that is light, and very little meat for my dinner. I have some biscuit and butter and a glass of sherry in the middle of the day, and just a piece of toast with my tea.

While I am writing, there is a Court Martial assembled at the opposite table to try two or three privates who have been misbehaving themselves. One man appears to have been selling his boots or doing something of that sort and, from the men's own account, they seem to have been always in prison when they committed their various offences.

We took in two passengers at Gibraltar, one of whom is a Frenchman, a curious individual who is perpetually sea-sick, and will never eat anything. He has not left the deck since he came on board so that he has neither washed nor taken his clothes off since Tuesday.

We have just had a test of the state of discipline on board, the alarm bell suddenly sounding long and loud, and all the troops rushing on deck in a frantic state, the men all in their quarters for muster in one minute, while some people were calling out "Fire" and others "She's sinking". It was merely to place the men at their fire and boat stations, and put them through their exercises and to see in how short a time they would be at their places. Most of the passengers in the saloon, who were writing, rushed up on deck to see what was the matter. I kept my seat and did not move till I knew what it was all about, and then I could afford to chaff some of those who had been in such a state of excitement.

7pm. It is coming on to blow a gale of wind from the north-west and all is being made snug for a dirty night.

February 21st

Gale of wind all night and still continuing with heavy rain and high sea, ship like a cork in a millstream. Very doubtful when we shall make Malta, very likely we shall not be able to till the gale moderates. Everything that is not fast is tumbling about and I nearly got sent out of bed last night. The saloon cabins are hot and close from being shut up and it is impossible to go on deck.

February 22nd

The weather was so bad that we were unable to have Divine Service on board, and altogether it was not too comfortable, as on deck one was drenched through with rain, and below it was so close that it was not bearable for any length of time, all the ports being closed, and the hatches battened down. They were unable to take observations, and we were knocking about all day in this storm, not knowing the least where we were, so different to last Sunday.

At last about five o'clock poor Capt. Powell, who looked like a drowned rat more than anything else (as he was thoroughly encased in mackintosh with a sort of bearskin cap), as he was standing close to me, with his double-barrelled looking glass up to his eye, sung out, "There's Gozo Light, Port!!! Turn ahead, full speed", upon which there was a regular Kentish trio of hurrahs all through the ship, and the engines, which had been kept at half-speed nearly all day, were turned on ahead full, and in about three and a half hours we were abreast of Gozo Light, which is about twenty miles from Valletta. We then steamed on for Valletta Light, which is just visible from Gozo, and when about twelve miles off exchanged rockets and blue lights with the *Valetta* with the homeward India mail, which we were very sorry to find as we just missed her to take over letters, but as there is a steamer from Malta to Marseilles of some sort or another nearly every day, it will not, I hope, make very much difference.[13]

We hove to soon after and sent up rockets and blue lights for a pilot, but could not get attended to, as the natives were afraid to come out in such a sea, so after sending up signals twice without reply, Captain Powell determined to run the ship in himself without one.

The whole coast of Malta and Gozo is very ugly-looking to have under a ship's lee in a gale. Large rocks without any beach, and a tremendous surf breaking all along. If our engines had by any chance given way, no power on earth could have saved us from being dashed to pieces, but the good old ship kept nobly on, though frequently one paddle wheel was five or six feet out of water, and the other proportionately immersed, and the figurehead was sometimes right under water, while at others the bottom of the forefoot was as dry as when she was on stocks. As she made sudden transitions from one position to another, standing on deck was not too easy, and walking quite out of the question. Luckily the rain went away as the sun went down so that, except occasional seas which drenched us well, we were not so badly off on deck, where I was as well as most of the gentlemen who were not ill.

The sight of the surf breaking on the rocks is immensely grand but when one reflects that the mere breaking of a rope or a piece of iron will send the ship without doubt right on to them, it rather changes the feeling of admiration into one of fear. However, we arrived safely at the entrance of the Quarantine Harbour, just as it struck seven bells (half past eleven) and then came the most difficult part; fancy a place about the third the width of Portsmouth Harbour at the entrance, with rocks on each side, and a heavy surf breaking right in, added to which instead of opening out wide as Portsmouth does, it continues in a sort of zigzag.

When we came abreast of the lighthouse we fired a gun, which seemed to rouse them for they did actually condescend to acknowledge it by letting off some blue lights. The ship was taken in in the most beautiful manner possible, with not ten yards at one part between us and the rocks on the port side. There are several experienced sailors on board, and they all said it was a most masterly piece of navigation. We were anchored safely just before eight bells, and I am sure we must all be most heartily thankful to Almighty God that he preserved us in the midst of so many dangers. Few turned in till she was safe at anchor. I was on deck nearly all day, except at meal times; not that I was the least frightened for I rather enjoyed the storm (barring the rain) while we had lots of sea room, and even when we were close inshore I reflected that we had a good ship and a good captain, and that none of the company's ships had ever been lost there before, and above all that there was a Power on high which would protect us in the midst of everything, so that I really hardly thought anything about the danger till we were safely at anchor.

Directly we were fast to the buoy all the Harbour seemed alive with coal barges coming alongside, and the natives made noise enough to float a 74. Nevertheless, I managed to get some sleep, and about quarter before six this morning Capt. Bayley and I turned out to make the most of our time on shore, as we were posted to leave at ten.

We had a cup of coffee before we started, and finding three others going on shore, took a boat together, for which we only paid 1/- (the proper fare), much to the disgust of the boatmen, who followed us over half the town expecting to fleece the strangers. They are curious sorts of boats, a sort of caique painted in the most gaudy manner; some I saw painted like a Yankee Jack, blue with white stars, others to imitate the waves, and others with a judicious mixture of red, blue, gilt and the most gaudy colours they could find.

Immediately on landing, we were beset by no end of natives telling us that they were the men to shew us over the place, etc., etc. However, the only way is to be very short and demonstrative with them, and even then it is not too easy to get rid of them, as they meet you at every corner of the street. Our three friends were nailed, but as Capt. Bayley knew the place and how to deal with them, we got away.

We took a walk through the principal streets and looked over the Grand Harbour, where there are several English lines of battle-ships and war steamers, which looked quite familiar. We then walked all through the town, looking at the principal buildings, and seeing all there was to be seen in so short a time, which was not very much.

The Cathedral, however, is a most splendid place, most gorgeously decorated inside and the pavement in it is something superb. I did not very much admire the exterior; it is, I think, a sort of Moorish architecture, but the decorations inside must have cost an immense sum of money. There were, of course, numbers of Maltese inside praying and telling their beads before their patron saints but we were too late for the Matins Mass.

I was rather struck with the wording of an inscription on one of the principal buildings in Malta:- MAGNAE ET INVICTAE BRITANNIAE MELITENSIUM AMOR ET EUROPAE VOX HAS INSULAS CONFIRMAVIT. A.D. 1814.[14] Sinclair will translate it for you if you cannot make it out.[15] I don't think there seems to be very much "Love for the Maltese" there, as everyone abuses them right and left.

I forgot to say that we arrived with the milk, which does not mean seeing a sturdy girl with a yoke on her shoulders and a pailful of chalk and water on each side but a man or woman (as the case may be) with a flock of goats, perhaps five and twenty, going to all the houses and milking the goat into a jug at the door. It looks rather curious, and one certainly has the advantage of getting pure milk. I do not believe there is such a thing as a cow in the island.

Malta is a curious place. The houses and all the buildings are built of a sort of sandstone or lava which I should think must be very glaring in a hot sun, and the streets are many of them steps up which it would be as easy to drive a carriage as to lead a cow up a ladder. There is a figure of some saint at nearly every corner and a great many of the Virgin Mary are sprinkled about in different parts of the town.

I was rather surprised at the smallness of the harbours in Malta, but they run deep close in to the shore like that of Sevastopol, and are very well fortified indeed, though I should think they are building new fortifications now. If we had had any longer there, we could have taken horses and ridden out to the catacombs, but had not the time for anything of that sort.

February 23rd

The *Euxine* arrived in harbour just as we were going on shore, not having ventured to come in the night before, and all the P&O letters were delivered just before we left. Capt. Bayley got a letter and an "Overland Mail" from the office. The latter was a great acquisition. Up to the time of our getting out of sight of Malta, nothing had been seen or heard of the *Teviot*, so we shall have the pleasure of beating her, in spite of our being hove to for twelve hours.

Poor Captain Powell was thoroughly knocked up yesterday, not having left the deck for ten minutes from Saturday morning till we were safe in Malta, and directly we got well clear of the place, he turned in and made his appearance again this morning all right again.

Tonight we have been drawing lots for the vans in the desert.[16] Our party consists of Captains Balfour and Hopkins of the Indian Navy, one a Scotchman, who can argue black white or any topic from mesmerism to the steam engine, and the other a regular Pat, with a strong rich brogue, who amuses all by his bolls and dry remarks, Captain Bayley, the two boys and myself. Captain Balfour said it would have been better to have had a lady, but we none of us knew any of the ladies well, and besides he said the two boys will take up so much less room.

I shall really be very sorry to leave the *Ripon* for we have been very jolly on board her and now I am beginning to get thoroughly used to it.

Today and yesterday have been two of the finest days I ever saw and now we begin to see a little of the beauty of the Mediterranean. The water is a beautiful deep blue and the sunrise and sunset are as beautiful sights as man ever beheld.

We left Malta exactly at ten, and the *Euxine* left about an hour after us, but by dinner time she was even with us, about two miles to the south, and those who were up early enough this morning were just able to discern her

13

masts above the horizon. She will be at Alexandria most probably half a day before us.

One of the passengers on board has got a sort of wideawake hat, which he bought at Calcutta, and he says we shall all wear hats like it at Bombay. It is made of pith, very light but thick, and looks something like a cross between an apple pudding and a lifebuoy. We have been laughing at him as he came on deck in it today and several have asked him if it would keep him up if he was thrown overboard. It looks as though it were meant to be inflated.

Captain Balfour, who is a knowing hand, says that this time he has taken everything out with him from England as, in consequence of the number of troops at Bombay, everything is much dearer than it has ever been known before. I think as far as I can judge from the other passengers, I seem to have hit the golden mean. Some have next to nothing, and had to buy collars at Malta, while others again have enough for half a dozen old maids and a newly married couple and have to pay I don't know what for extra baggage, much to their disgust.[17]

February 24th

Weather today has been very cold and everybody is putting on greatcoats and all sorts of wrappers to go on deck. The wind has been abeam and the ship rolling a great deal, keeping the ladies who came on board at Malta in their cabins. In fact, two have not yet made their appearance.

One of the passengers has lent me a book called "Arundines Cami" and I have been busy all day copying extracts into my book.[18]

February 25th

This is a delightful morning and now for the first time I see the real beauty of the Mediterranean. The water was blue after we left Malta but it is now a much deeper blue, and the sky ditto.

They are getting up all the baggage from the hold and cabins today and I shall say "Good-bye".

NOTES

1. At this time, passengers would sail from Southampton to Alexandria. Here they disembarked and travelled overland to Suez where they joined another ship for India. At the time Kendall is writing, a railway was being built across the desert but the final twenty-five miles had to be undertaken by horse-drawn vans.

2. Ship's hulks were strategically positioned by P&O to store coal and other essential

supplies. At many ports, in the absence of proper quays or berths, ships came alongside the hulks and passengers were ferried ashore by boat.

3. Mr. Paine was a General Manager of P&O in London.

4. Tiffin was a light meal which ultimately came to be regarded as lunch.

5. Rhubarb pills, essentially a mild laxative, were regarded as something of a panacea until recent times.

6. The early steam ships still carried a full set of sails which were used, where possible, to reduce fuel consumption.

7. Until 1871, the mails were accompanied by Admiralty Agents who were retired or half-pay Naval officers. Their function was to safeguard the mails and ensure that the ships were operated to agreed schedules.

8. P&O's first ships were manned by officers recruited from the Royal Navy and The Honourable East India Company and, consequently, many of the working practices and terminology were naval in origin. P&O sea staff still quote their old maxim that "There is the Royal Navy, the P&O and the Merchant Navy".

9. *Ripon's* voyage was an additional sailing to carry troops out to India to help to suppress the Mutiny.

10. "The other side" refers to the steamship route east of Suez, i.e. the other side of Suez.

11. The success of the early steamers depended upon the all-important mail contracts which could be withdrawn if the ships did not consistently meet the agreed schedules. For this reason, there was intense rivalry between the companies to demonstrate their ships were faster and more reliable, etc.

12. No more than a day or two's supply of fresh meat could be carried in the days before refrigeration and supplies were, in the main, carried salted or 'on the hoof'. P&O's practice was to ship sufficient livestock for the journey from Southampton to Alexandria and back. Fresh provisions for ships going on to the East were taken on in Egypt, where P&O maintained its own farm and stores. The pony was likely to have been carried as cargo.

13. Before wireless communications, messages between ship and shore were by means of rockets, coloured flares, semaphore signals and cannon.

14. This inscription on the Main Guard of the Palace Square in Valletta reads, "The affection of the Maltese people and the voice of Europe has confirmed these islands to great and invincible Britain. A.D. 1814."

15. Sinclair was Kendall's younger brother who, after schooling, also joined P&O.

16. For the journey across the desert, horse-drawn vans were arranged by P&O. Drawing lots to form little parties was one of the ways of passing the time prior to arrival in Egypt. Not everyone wished to travel with the ladies since their voluminous dresses took up so much room in the small vans.

17. A packing list of the time for a properly equipped lady included 24 day chemises, 12 night chemises, 4 dressing gowns, 6 pair kid gloves, 24 pair fine thread stockings and 12 pair of silk stockings, 4 bonnets, 6 gowns, 1 opera cloak, green and blue veils, riding habit and hat and a life preserver. Recommendations for a gentleman included 40 shirts, 12 waistcoats, 30 pair of cotton hose, 12 pair of gloves, turban hat and helmet, one blue or green veil, 1 tweed suit, 1 dress suit, 1 frock coat, 2 fancy trousers, 5 jackets, and a corkscrew.

18. Arundines Cami, or Reeds of the Cam, was published in 1841 and was a collection of English verse translated into Latin verse by several Cambridge scholars.

15

THE OVERLAND ROUTE.

(FROM A CORRESPONDENT.)

ADEN, MARCH 12.

Before this reaches London you will have doubtless heard more than one account of the late disagreeable affair at Suez, connected with the despatch of a detachment of Her Majesty's 92d Highlanders, under Colonel Mackenzie, to Bombay. That any such *fracas* should have occurred on the overland route is very much to be regretted, and it is to be hoped that a sifting inquiry will be instituted in order to discover who are the culprits on either side in this most shameful business.

Though not present on the occasion, I have thought that a plain statement of the facts, as related to me by three of the passengers who were on board the Pottinger at the time, and who have no connexion whatever with either party, might be useful in enabling the public at home to form a correct judgment of what actually transpired.

It appears, then, that the Pottinger, having been ordered to convey a detachment of troops to Bombay, took in at Suez sufficient provisions for 320 men for 28 days. The detachment had not reached Suez on the 27th, and the commander, it appears, foreseeing that the men would not be comfortable if permitted to come on board while the expected cargo was being taken in, suggested to the authorities at Suez the propriety of their being embarked on board the hulk Zenobia (where ample accommodation was provided) until the steamer was quite ready to receive them. For some reason, however, this prudent suggestion was overruled, and the men were embarked on board the Pottinger late that evening. Grog was immediately served out to them, but the men had no beds, it having been reported to the captain that the men's bedding would be sent with them. Some disagreeableness is said to have arisen at this early stage between the purser of the vessel and the colonel, the latter being very much chagrined that an entire cabin had not been reserved for him, instead of his being made to occupy a cabin with Colonel Anderson, one of the passengers. During the night the cargo arrived, and one can easily conceive that the men were not comfortable under such circumstances, without beds, as they were, and a cold wind blowing.

Next day a complaint was made about the biscuit, and it turned out that a cask which had been on board for two or three months had been served out. This was soon rectified, and no further complaints made on that head.

Shortly after noon the colonel and several of the officers, attended by some of the men carrying a plate of pork, complained to the captain that it was bad, rotten, and unfit for use. The captain, we hear, declared that it was perfectly sound; but the colonel maintained the contrary, and further, that he would not allow his men to go to sea with the prospect of being fed on such rations. An order was then given by the mail agent to detain the ship until a committee was held on the stores. Four casks were immediately hoisted up, during which operation it appears that an ensign of the regiment applied a most offensive epithet to the officer superintending the operations, who was otherwise subjected to the muttered abuse of the soldiers. From all I can learn, the verdict of the officers forming the committee was not unanimous; but the general opinion appears to have been that the colonel was satisfied. My informants did not speak with certainty on this point, and were themselves divided in opinion about the quality of the provisions. It seems, however, that the conduct of the men during the inquiry was familiar in the extreme towards their own officers.

Matters being so far settled, the order was given to prepare for sea, when the hitherto muttered discontent of the men broke out into open insubordination. The Lascars who attempted to weigh the anchor were thrown off the forecastle, and the officers on duty abused and threatened by the men, who armed themselves with bars, bolts, and whatever they could lay hands on, swearing that they would take the cabins, and burn the ship, &c. The colonel went forward, but it does not appear that his visit effected any good. What was next to be done? I hear that it was proposed for 100 of the men to be left behind in the hulk, and to come on by the next steamer, but the colonel would not assent to that arrangement. Finally, during the night the men were taken from the Pottinger, and embarked on board the Columbian, bound first for Aden and Galle. Immediately after the mail agent ordered the captain of the Pottinger to start with the mails, when a requisition was brought off by the Transit steamer for the provisions to be sent on board the Columbian (the provisions which had been condemned previously), but the captain was not authorized to wait, and, knowing that stores of the same kind were procurable in abundance at Suez, the Pottinger sailed at once for Aden.

The foregoing is a brief outline of this sad affair, and it is sincerely to be hoped that such measures will be taken in this case as will effectually prevent a recurrence of anything so disgraceful. A great error was made at the outset by those who disregarded the advice of Captain Stead, of the Pottinger, that the men should be lodged for the night in the hulk. If I am not mistaken, the Pottinger, under Captain Stead, was considered a pattern trooper, and was quite a favourite with the Europeans during the Persian war, when she must have carried many more men than there were in the detachment of the 92d. Of course, it is impracticable that on board a mail and passenger boat men can have the same accommodation as on board a troopship; but whatever accommodation there was must have appeared less, and have been far less available at nighttime, and while the ship's decks were being encumbered with cargo, &c. Hitherto, indeed, nothing could have gone on more smoothly than the trooping to India by this route, even in vessels of less tonnage than the Pottinger; and it is very much to be deplored that any such *contretemps* as this should have taken place. Of course, if it is found, after due inquiry, that the provisions were bad, the Peninsular and Oriental Company should be severely dealt with ; but even if that at present debateable point is proved against them such a result will in no way exculpate the insubordinate conduct of the men, and the reported *insouciance* of their officers in repressing it. On these latter points, indeed, the evidence appears concurrent and unanimous—so much so, indeed, that when the Pottinger reached Aden several of the passengers had decided to remain here should the Columbian reach before she left, and the troops be ordered to re-embark in her.

2 Extract from The Times of 31 March, 1858

16

2
Overland: Alexandria to Suez

February 28th, 1858

We arrived off Alexandria at midnight on Thursday, and went into harbour at daylight on Friday morning. At eight o'clock everybody went on shore, and all the passengers except two left behind, with the exception of Capt. Bayley and myself, went at once to the Railway Station and started for Suez. The troops were to leave at four o'clock in the afternoon, and so Mr. Holton said that Capt. Bayley and myself might as well stay and spend the day with them, and go forward with the troops.[1] We accordingly went up to Mr. Holton's and had a second breakfast and a chat with Mrs. Holton, and took a couple of donkeys, and rode off to the Pasha's Palace.

You must know that in Alexandria, whenever anybody wants to go anywhere they hire a donkey. We started off with a black fellow behind each and rode up to the palace. The first thing on entering, we had to take off our boots, and were supplied with a pair of loose slippers, and then we walked all through the palace. The rooms are most magnificently decorated, and the floors inlaid, some with polished wood and others with ebony and ivory. The walls are covered with silk instead of paper, and all the furniture is most gorgeous. The bedsteads are solid silver and everything else is in a corresponding style, but I thought many things were in bad taste. Altogether I thought it seemed a very great waste of money and to very little purpose.

After distributing a due amount of "Bucksheesh" to the attendants, we wended our way back again. The donkeys go very well but the saddles are of curious formation with a great hump in front, and the stirrups are run right through so that if you bear more heavily on one side than the other, down you go. Most of the people there do not use the stirrups at all. I found it was no use trying to rise to the motion of the donkey but that the only way was to sit well back as hard as possible.

Alexandria is a curious place. The streets are narrow and the houses, generally speaking, very badly built. The place, of course, swarms with Arabs and you see them squatting down on their heels with their chins between their knees, smoking and talking. They do not touch the ground

17

with their body generally, and how they can balance themselves in that posture, I can't conceive.

We had some lunch at the Holtons' and left about half past three. The Holtons have very nice apartments indeed. They all live in "go-downs" or flats like Victoria Street and the Holtons are on the first floor and have very large airy rooms.

We had given the donkeymen 1/6d for the two of us, which was about three times what they would have got from a resident, but they wanted some more, and waited about the place till we came out in the afternoon, and then one of them came up holding out his hand and calling out "Bucksheesh". Mr. Holton said to us that we had given him more than his fare, and so he was not content without more still, but he just made a sign to his man, and he went inside his office, and returned with a long piece of flexible cowhide at the sight of which the man went away as fast as his legs would carry him.[2]

When we got to the Railway, we found the troops getting into the carriages. They had all smock frocks and large white linen cap covers with long lappets to protect them from the sun. They all went into second class carriages, which are as good as almost any first class in England, and the officers and such of us as had not gone forward in the morning went in first class, which are the finest carriages I have ever been in. We had a long train, as all the baggage, etc., went in it, and we did not make much more than twelve miles an hour. We did not start till five, and then went steadily on. Every time the train stopped I expected to hear "Lewisham" or "Num 'Dnum", i.e., Sydenham. It was so like being in dear old England.

The country all the way to Cairo is very fertile but flat and uninteresting. The principal trees are the date-palms, which look as though some giant housemaid had taken a number of feather dustbrushes and stuck them into the ground. We stopped at several stations, some of them merely a place to water the engine, but all the others which had any building at all had a long stone house with perhaps twenty large rooms which were as far as we could make out of no earthly use, as there was nobody in any of them, except perhaps a few Arabs who knew nothing whatever about the train, but just went in there to smoke and talk.

We crossed the Nile at Kafr Azizat in a sort of floating bridge which deserves description. It was about fifty feet above the water, the platform of the bridge being made to go up and down, so as to be on a level with the railway at all times of tide. As we were going on board one of the soldiers nearly lost his life. There was a space about three feet long and one board between the bridge and the shore, and one of the men fell down this. Luckily he held on like grim death till he was picked up. If he had gone through he could not possibly have been heard of again, as there was a fall of fifty feet, and the current running very strong below. The bridge took five carriages and all the men over at the first trip, and whilst they were bringing the rest of the train across we went and had some supper.

The men were uncommonly well fed: they had tea and coffee, Irish stews, and all sorts of meat, bread and vegetables. We also did very well with a turkey and ducks, goat, fowls, etc., and puddings afterwards, besides as much ale as we chose to drink and as many oranges as we chose to take.

We left Kafr Azizat about half past five the next morning. The other passengers were sleeping at Cairo and we caught them up and went on before them. I made myself very comfortable, putting on my pea jacket and putting my legs up on the opposite seat, well covered up with my rug, as it was pretty cold. Capt. Bayley was not in the same compartment, but Whiteley was, as well as the doctor of the troops who were at the other side of the carriage, and two Arabs. What woke us first of all was one of these men blowing tremendous clouds of smoke from his chibouque, and all the windows being shut. We immediately opened them, much to his disgust, as he was getting comfortable. He could not talk to us but he looked; however, we were not going to be suffocated for him. He looked amazed when we undid our carpet bags, and took out sundry combs and brushes and began putting our hair to rights, and evidently could not make out the least what we were doing when we began bathing our faces with eau de Cologne, as being the best substitute for washing.

We could not see much of the pyramids from the railway except for a distant glimpse. We did not stop more than ten minutes at Cairo and there was no place where we could wash. We stopped to take in water about half past six at a place where there was a small pond, and I immediately rushed out with towel and soap and got a good wash, which was the most refreshing I think I have ever had, though at the expense of getting my ankles in mud.

At half past nine we came to No.12 Station, the end of the Railway, where we disembarked and had a good breakfast, and then came the best fun of the day, seeing the soldiers all mount their donkeys.[3] The officers shewed them how to mount first of all, and the largest man amongst them, much to the amusement of everybody. The donkeys are all very small and the men very large, and they could generally almost walk, though they were astride. The poor unfortunate animals (unless they broke down, which was the case with several) had to convey them the whole twenty-five miles to Suez along a road where generally the hot sand was over their fetlocks. In England a man would be taken up for cruelty to animals if he rode one of them for half a mile, but here they think nothing of it, and there is even a boy or man to run behind each donkey the whole way.

We left No.12 Station at eleven o'clock. The officers all rode with the men, but there were three vans prepared: one for us, the others for the small baggage and sick. The vans are externally something like the "Fairy" on two wheels or a carrier's cart, but they are not uncomfortable inside, though of course there is a great deal of jolting. They are drawn by two mules in the shafts, and two horses on ahead.

We stopped and got some lunch at a place about twelve miles from Suez; of course we went much faster than the troops, and were there by ourselves. We arrived at Suez at three, and went to the Hotel first of all and got another good wash, and then reconnoitred the place till six when the troops arrived, and we went straight on board the steamer, and came out to the *Pottinger*. She has, as you will see, come up after all instead of the *Madras,* the latter vessel being in dock at Bombay. We had some dinner and got into our cabins before the other passengers arrived about nine o'clock. The ship is quite full.

NOTES

1. Mr. Holton was P&O's Agent in Alexandria.

2. An apparently effective solution at that time! See also his entry for 30th June, 1858.

3. P&O originally built rest-houses, or stations, across the desert to enable passengers to rest for a few minutes while horses were changed. The original route was substantially followed by the railway and some of the rest-houses were still in use many years later.

3 A Desert Rest House.

20

3
On Board "Pottinger"

February 28th, 1858

Capt. Bayley and I are in a large cabin in the forepart of the ship with two others. It is a very large airy cabin, and I doubt not we shall be very comfortable. The clerk in charge of this ship I know very well, having been in the office in London with him. The luggage came on board all right this morning at eight o'clock without my having had the least bother or trouble with it at all.

It is most curious to see the Arabs working on board ship. They work so uncommonly early and as if they were in no hurry about it. Instead of the "Noise yoi hee" of our sailors in hauling, they all sing together with pauses between something which sounds like "Allyar maimar", and instead of the "Tshick" in driving they call out "Hi Hi".

9 p.m. We should have started this morning but there has been a mutiny of the soldiers on board and the Captain will not put to sea with them, so they are all going to leave the ship and go down as far as Aden in the *Columbian*. All particulars from Aden.[1]

March 1st

Yesterday was the most eventful day we have had since we left Southampton, and it has ended in all the troops being taken out of the ship and making us a great deal more comfortable in every way.

As I told you yesterday, the troops came on board about seven on Saturday evening, and as the *Pottinger* is not nearly so commodious a ship as the *Ripon*, they had to be berthed on deck, much the same as they would in an ordinary troop ship. This they did not like, after having been treated so well on board the *Ripon*, and they appeared rather discontented at it. The officers too were not too well pleased, as they had not whole cabins given to them, which I suppose they expected because they had been so well off on board the *Ripon*, but which they could not possibly have here in justice to the other passengers.

The *Pottinger* is a very comfortable ship and has beautiful large airy cabins, larger even than the *Ripon*, and I am sure that nobody in their senses could have any cause to complain, only I suppose they think with Naval officers that they have a right to everything.

However, when the men had their dinner yesterday at one o'clock, some of them complained that the pork was bad. I did not taste the pork myself so cannot positively say anything about it, but Capt. Curling did and he says that he wishes he may always have as good himself. Upon hearing the men complain, the Colonel requested that a survey might be held upon the provisions, which was accordingly done, and they turned out in beautiful order. Out of the many casks that there were opened, there was one cask of beef from which the salt had oozed away a little at the top, and the meat in that cask at the top was not in so good condition as the rest, but still not at all bad, and the rest was really beautiful meat, such as one does not very often see, all the prime parts of the meat, thoroughly well salted and in the best possible condition. Indeed the company pay for it £15 a tierce more than they do for their own sailors, about which there has never been a single complaint, but when men are determined to grumble, they will do so at anything. If they got half as good meat from the Commissariat, they would think themselves very well off.

The Colonel was in a most excited state, and was holding forth before the men, I think very unwisely. He found that he could not possibly make any complaint about the quality of the provisions, and then he turned round and accused the Purser of having only six days' provisions on board. The Purser told him that he had got provisions for a month. "Why," said he, "you have on 26 half casks, and there is only 50lbs to the tierce." "Well," said the Purser, "we reckon 200lbs and 300lbs to the tierce, according as they are beef or pork." "Oh," said the Colonel, "I saw 50 marked on the cask and so thought it was 50lbs." The Purser then explained that it meant 50 four pound pieces, upon which the Colonel was satisfied.

It was then four o'clock in the afternoon, and if they did not sail at once they must wait till two o'clock in the morning, as they are obliged to pass through the Straits of Jabal in daylight, so the men were sent to weigh anchor. Immediately the troops rushed up on to the forecastle, and seized the hand spikes, hauled them out of the capstan, began belabouring some of the Lascars, and threatened to throw anyone overboard who went near the capstan.[2]

The Colonel and all the officers went forward, but had no more authority over them than a deal board. He, the Colonel, told them to go down off the forecastle. "We won't go," they sung out, "We'll burn the .... ship, and every person on board", and sending other remarks of a similar nature. The Colonel then came aft, but instead of calling a muster of the men, as one

22

would naturally expect he would have done as they were not all in this mutinous state, he took a boat and went off to the shore and made arrangements for taking the troops away on board the *Columbian.*

The Captain of the ship, Captain Stead, refused to put to sea with the men in that state and the Admiralty Agent, Lieut. Morrell, sanctioned his delaying the ship. The Captain and Admiralty Agent then went on board the *Columbian* and consulted with the Captain and Admiralty Agent and the Colonel, and they also telegraphed, I believe, to Colonel Pocklinton at Cairo. The result was however that the men were removed on board the *Columbian*, and half of them left this ship about half past one a.m. and the other half, half an hour afterwards on Monday, much to the relief of all the passengers and officers on the ship.

Just as we were heaving up the anchor, and were nearly ready to sail, at two thirty a.m. the Colonel sent his compliments to Captain Stead, and "Would he let them have the provisions?". Captain Stead sent his compliments in return and said that all the men were busy getting up the anchor and that he was behind his time then; he dare not delay the ship another half hour, unless the Admiralty Agent would give him leave to detail the ship till four o'clock the next day, which the Admiralty Agent declined to do unless Capt. Stevens, the Admiralty Agent of the *Columbian*, would take the responsibility of it, because of course every hour is precious when the mails are on board, and there were plenty of provisions to be got from the shore. We then got under way, and the *Columbian* blew off steam, and prepared to remain till the next day.

I think the men have got "out of the frying-pan into the fire" as, though the *Columbian* is a very much larger ship, her accommodation is very bad, and there is no room for them on deck, it being all lumbered up with deckhouses, while below they will be stifled. The Colonel too, I expect, will get into hot water, as he has taken the whole responsibility of moving the men upon himself, and they will find that the *Pottinger* has frequently taken 800 or 900 men, and has taken 500 on deck, and that they have always been very comfortable. In fact nearly all the soldiers who went from England to the Crimea went as deck passengers in the cold weather, and they are all supposed to be conveyed on deck; only when we have room we take them below, on the other side, but here many of the passengers sleep on deck in preference, and by the time (March 2nd) they would have complained that they were stifled had they been below.

I cannot help thinking the Colonel was to blame in giving way to them as he did, instead of putting some of them under arrest at once, and in fact all the officers gave way to them completely, except Capt. Newall who said he would put twenty or thirty of them in irons directly he got them to Bombay. The *Columbian* is not going to Bombay; she will only be able to take them as far as Aden, unless they go on to Galle, and then I don't know how they will get to Bombay. I am quite sure that had the Colonel sounded the bugle for the men to fall in, at least two-thirds of them would have done it and it would have been easy to put the others under arrest, but he only said, "Now my men, go down, go down", and when they wouldn't, he did. He is an extremely nice man to talk to, but it does not seem as if he knew at all how to command his men.

We are not at all sorry to get rid of them out of the ship, as you may suppose, but I do not think they care to have them on board the other except that it will be a windfall for the E. & A. Co. getting their passage money, if they get down safely.[3] There was nothing really to complain of here, except that they had not brought their blankets with them, and we are just as comfortable as we were on board the *Ripon* in every way. Now the officers have gone, Capt. Bayley and I have got the cabin to ourselves. It is a large cabin, and about twice the size of the one we had in the *Ripon*, so we are well off.

The old *Pottinger* is considered the slowest ship on this side, except the *Linwood* and *Trecinsor* which do not go down to sea, but since we left Suez we have been bowling along, sometimes going twelve and a half knots, and averaging over eleven, with a fair wind and studding sails set "alow and aloft".

We carried away our main topgallant studding sail last night, and one of the passengers, a Dr. Kelland, who came via Marseilles and seems a great muff, got into a tremendous fright, thought the ship was going on shore and sinking or something of the sort, was rushing madly about, shaking hands with people and telling one or two to stick together and form a European crew for a boat, then getting out his knife and rushing out to cut a boat away, and then seeing the Captain, remonstrated with him for carrying so much sail, and asked all the officers and everybody whether they really thought there was much danger. Of course the answers he got did not encourage him, as one man told him there was a fire in the engine room, and another pointed to the light which had just been sent up the foremast head, and called it a signal of distress, and so on. The ladies too were chaffing him right and left, and he got in such a fright that he did not take off his clothes at all last night. Today he seems alright again, but if it comes on to blow at all, I dare say he will be just as bad again.

24

We have three cows and three calves on board. Two of them are Aden cows and are I think the handsomest I ever saw. One is perfectly white, and they are both so tame that you may do anything to them. They are rather different to our English cows, having a hump on the back of the neck.

The soldiers which were on board are the same about which there was such a row at Portsmouth just before we started.[4] I cannot see the least what there was for the Colonel or anybody else to complain of and when the matter comes to be investigated at home, which of course it will be, I do not think he will have a leg to stand on.

As yet we have not found it unpleasantly hot, at least I have not. I have hitherto gone without a waistcoat in the middle of the day, but wear my flannel shirts and make no other difference in my dress. Today at dinner we had the punkahs going, and nice and cool they made it.[5] The claret and iced water is uncommonly delicious.[6] We have two or three English stewards but most of them are natives, and are always called "Boys"; instead of calling "Steward", you call "Boy", although they are all of them men. The crew except the English Quartermaster are all Lascars. The stewards or boys dress in unexceptionable white jacket and shirt, and it looks rather curious to see an ebony-coloured face at the top.

Altogether the whole affair, coming through Egypt, and on board here, reminds me very much of a scene at the "Princess's", and one can hardly believe it is all real.[7] The crossing the Nile particularly was so, a dark night and the men in grotesque dresses, smock frocks and cap covers which are something after the style of a garden bonnet, and then the Arabs and Egyptians of every shade of colour, and all sorts of curious dresses coming as spectators, some of them bearing lights which consist of a sort of brazier or charcoal at the end of a long rod. There were some thousands of Arabs at work on the railway. They are obliged to work for, I think, seven weeks without any pay, but they get bread and water given to them and are sent back at the end of the time. As might be supposed, they do not work in a very lively manner, but crawl up and down like snails, talking the most clattering sound gibberish anybody ever heard and, now and again, sitting down to rest in their peculiar fashion.

It is most amusing too to see the way they guide the little steamer at Suez. Instead of running right alongside the ship at once they go along round and then make a shot at the ship, and invariably miss it, and then have to go round again and run alongside.

My journey through Egypt was most interesting and not all disagreeable, only I was rather tired at the end of it. I think we fared better than the other

25

passengers as they had a bit of a scramble for their meals, and we being only thirteen, and after the officers left us, only five, got on very comfortably.

March 3rd

The Red Sea, as far as I have at present seen it, is a deep blue colour, and very salty, as one finds out when having a bath, as, unless you have a can of fresh water poured on your head when you come out of the bath, your head gets quite full of salt and is sticky and uncomfortable.[8]

There is one great advantage in sleeping in the fore saloon: one has only to put on a pair of drawers or pyjamas and run up on deck, have a bath and run down again, without the chance of meeting any ladies en route.

We have a curious lot of passengers from Marseilles, none of them, I think, as far as I have seen, a very bright lot. There is a Colonel Anderson, a very dyspeptic livery-looking old Indian, with his wife, and two young daughters, who flirt with all the young men on board (all who will flirt with them) in the most barefaced manner; a Mr. Prirup and his wife, a newly married couple as affectionate as two turtle doves, and a lot of would-be fast young men, who smoke cigars and flirt with the Miss Andersons all day long, while the old mother looks on and seems to enjoy it. They are mostly in the civil service and I suppose she thinks that a young man worth £300 a year, dead or alive, is not to be sneezed at.

As I was waiting for my bath this morning while they were washing decks, they let the geese out as they do every morning and one of them got away and got out by the paddle box, and when one of the men went behind to catch him he flew overboard and swam away looking as contented as possible. Poor thing, I expect he will find his pond a little bigger than he expected.

I expect there will be a regular row at home about this affair with the troops; indeed, I do not well see how it can be otherwise, and I hope it may be so, because I am sure that they will be quite unable to find anybody connected with the P&O to blame. The Captain has requested all the officers of the ship to write and give him all particulars as far as they know, and he has asked me to make copies of their letters, which I shall be very glad to do, as it will be some amusement during the voyage.

I cannot hear that the *Cyclops* has arrived yet, but I think it is more than probable that we shall meet her at Aden.[9]

I have not shaved since I left, and my moustache is getting pretty well defined. Nobody seems to shave here; all the officers wear their beards.

March 5th

Yesterday was very hot, the thermometer being at 86. Today there is a head wind blowing pretty stiffly, so that it is not so hot. I find the best way to have a bath is to go when they are washing decks of a morning and have the hose brought into the bathroom to play upon me. It is glorious. Yesterday and today I have been busy making copies of the letters to send home to the Managing Directors.

I am woke in the morning about half past six by the steward, who brings a cup of tea and a biscuit, about seven or seven thirty I have my bath, breakfast at eight, at which I have a cup of tea or a glass of iced claret and water, and a little ham or something else light, a biscuit for tiffin at twelve, dinner at four, and a cup of tea about seven. I do not take any beer and scarcely ever any wine except claret.

March 6th

I suppose Sinclair will have returned to school by the time you get this. I shall be glad to know what you think of doing with him. I do not much think Purser line this side would suit him.

An immense shoal of small porpoises is now swimming along with the ship. They do look so curious jumping about. Thermometer about ninety in the cabin.

March 9th

We arrived at Aden the day before yesterday at one o'clock in the day. We should have been in the night before or early in the morning, if it had not been for a succession of strong head winds for the two days previous to our arrival.

The first news we heard on our arrival was not good: the loss of the *Ava*, one of the Company's steamers, with the Calcutta mail on board. Capt. Kirton had command of her. The whole thing is most unfortunate, as in addition to the ship being a dead loss of about £70,000 to the Company, they will probably have to pay for all the cargo and specie that has gone in her.[10] They say too that the officers' insurances won't hold good, as she was deviating from her regular course in going into Trincomalee. I am afraid Capt. Kirton will get in for it, but I hope he will be able to clear himself. What a state his old father will be in about it, and Mrs. Holton too.

One of our finest steamers, the *Alma*, has been lying at Aden for the last two months with her main shaft broken, and the *Ava* was bringing round a new shaft for her from Calcutta. Now she will have to wait till a new one has been made and sent out from England.

What with this and the comparatively small specie shipment lately, I expect the dividend will be something less than 15% this year, and probably the shares will go down a little, so that I expect it will be a good time to buy in.[11]

Nearly all the passengers went on shore soon after we arrived and took donkeys up to the "Camp", about 4 miles from the landing place.[12] I went with Lieut. Morrell the Admiralty Agent and young Duffin. We had sundry disputes with the natives about the fares, etc., as they of course wanted to cheat us right and left, but Mr. Morrell had been there before and knew what was proper, so every time they asked us for money we got down and walked a few yards till they soon brought the donkeys back and said we could leave the payment till we got back.

Aden is a barren-looking place. I should think it must be a horrid place to live in. From the sea it looks a little like Gibraltar only, I think, not nearly so grand and there are not half a dozen European houses to be seen anywhere. The natives are a curious-looking set of men, most of them reminding one very much of the pictures one sees in missionary tracts, but some of them are the most extraordinary-looking men I ever saw. They are quite black, and have their hair sticking out about a foot all round their head in regular long red strings, exactly like the red mops one sees hanging outside chandlers' shops. In fact one cannot believe it is hair. It looks much more as though it was meant to wipe one's feet on.

The donkeys go very well, and mine beat all of them. The natives would keep running on behind and belabouring the poor beasts although they were all going on capitally. I had not a stick with me, and so, after having sung out to them till I was hoarse to leave the poor beast alone, I gave every fellow that touched my donkey a punch on the head, so they soon left it alone, and the consequence was my donkey went ahead of them all though I had no stick to beat him with.

We walked through the native bazaar which is a filthy dirty place, and after investing in a bottle of lemonade each and giving our donkeys a rest, rode back again.

The natives all go naked except a piece of linen round their loins, and none of them think of wearing shoes; indeed on board, though we have a crew of about 160 Lascars and seedies and boys, I don't suppose there is a pair of shoes among them. There are three English Quartermasters and about half a dozen English stewards.

I had tea on board the *Alma* and went on board the *Pottinger* again about nine. We sailed at half past eleven, the *Columbian* not having made her appearance. If she had come in before we left, I expect we should have had to take the troops on board again. However, we have got nicely out of it, and I think it is not at all unlikely that they will have to do duty at Aden for some time, which will serve them quite right.

March 15th
Since leaving Aden we have sped very well, and I expect shall be in Bombay tomorrow afternoon or evening. Our voyage has been altogether a most pleasant one, and would have been even more so, had the young ladies been a little better behaved, but really the way they have been going on has been most scandalous, so that I almost wonder they have found any young men to flirt with them so long. For my own part I have not spoken to any of the three unmarried ladies, and I do not intend to. I never saw girls go on as they do, and they are not at all particular what they say either. Captain Bayley is thoroughly disgusted with them and so I think are most of the gentlemen in the ship.

The appearance of the *Pottinger* internally is a little different to the *Ripon*, the cabins being all made with venetians to them which can be opened so as to let the air through, and the punkahs slung over the dinner table look rather curious at first. She is also built with a poop and forecastle instead of flush like the *Ripon*.

We have a regular farmyard on board, as in addition to the cows we have about forty sheep and a gazelle, also a goat and kid. They are all great pets of mine; the sheep are very different to English sheep, being more like goats, only they have no horns. The gazelle is a great favourite. I think of various places in the morning when I wake, but principally of Shedfield, as the blacksmith's anvil is generally sounding in one's ears at that time and the cocks begin to crow, and the cows to low to be milked, the sheep and rabbits and all the animals are making various noises and requesting in their own peculiar ways that their breakfast may be got ready with as little delay as possible.[13]

16th March
I have just been witnessing the funeral of a dead cockroach. He had been crushed by something, and in about half an hour about a million little ants had congregated round him and walked him off, nearly as fast as he could walk himself had he been alive and well.[14]

NOTES

1. The incident Kendall describes created much comment in the British and Indian press. Although a Court of Enquiry found that the root cause, as Kendall later correctly suggests, was indiscipline, none of the offenders were court-martialled. In this they were fortunate, for the ringleader of a mutiny of troops on board *Jason* in March 1959, who used threatening language to an officer and who tried to lower a boat to leave the vessel, was sentenced to four years penal servitude and fifty lashes (later remitted).

2. Indian and Pakistani crews have been employed by P&O since 1842 and remain a traditional feature of many P&O ships.

3. *Columbian* was owned by the Eastern & Australian Steamship Company. The ship and the company were later acquired by P&O.

4. I have not been able to trace details of any disturbance at Portsmouth. Possibly the men were boisterous the night before embarking.

5. Punkahs were oblong fans suspended from the deckhead and waved to and fro by mechanical means to create a cooling draught.

6. The P&O Company stocked its own brand of claret which was renowned for its quality. In hot climates, chilled claret and iced water was considered to make a light refreshing drink.

7. Thought to be the Princess Theatre in Portsmouth.

8. The early ships carried limited quantities of fresh water. Baths were, therefore, taken in sea-water and, when possible, followed by a quick dousing of fresh water.

9. Use of the Electric Telegraph was now rapidly spreading. England and France were connected by a telegraph cable in 1851, and by 1858 *Cyclops* was making surveys to carry the cable from England to India by way of the Red Sea. James Allan, Managing Director of P&O, was on the Board of the Electric Telegraph Company.

10. Specie. A term covering cargoes of coin or precious metals such as gold.

11. Despite the financial crisis caused by the virtual cessation of cargoes of silk to and specie from China, the usual dividend of four and a half percent was declared for the first half year.

12. The Camp was the site of the first encampment of the British troops after Aden was occupied in 1839.

13. Kendall's family originally came from Cornwall and moved to Hampshire when Edward Kendall retired from the Navy and joined P&O. The illusion of being in the country must soon have been strengthened by the odours emanating from the livestock pens, particularly in hot or bad weather.

14. This is most likely to have been written ashore.

4
At Bombay

March 18th, 1858

We arrived at 6.30 p.m. on Tuesday, but I did not go on shore that night. Yesterday I went to the office and was put in harness at once. There is an extra mail going out today, so have an opportunity of sending this, but I have not got the time to write any particulars as the mail closes at once, and I shall have a lot of Company's letters to write this morning. A long letter in a week's time, by the next mail.

March 20th

I had only time by the last mail to put a scrap on to the end of my letter to say I was here. Now I will try to give you a few particulars.

When about thirty miles off Bombay, we saw several snakes swimming about on top of the water, good-sized fellows which sundry persons mistook for young sea serpents, but which they say are very common and that they can tell the distance the ship is off by the size of the snakes. Soon after the water gradually changed colour, till from being a deep blue it became the colour and consistency of Thames water. Then we bid a fond adieu to porpoises and flying fish, to dolphins and ocean, and hailed the rapidly-approaching land with new feelings of interest. We took in a Pilot and threaded our way in through the ships and anchored off the Apollo Bunda just about a mile off the Fort.

Many of the passengers went on shore at once, and among them Captain Bayley. I did not know whether Mr. Ritchie would want me there, so I quietly slept on board, as did also some of the other passengers.[1]

One man was in such a hurry to get into a boat that he stepped overboard, which rather cooled his ardour. Luckily, he was a good swimmer, so he only got a ducking and came on board again to change, when he again made the attempt with a little better success.

The first thing after breakfast in the morning, I went on shore with Mr. Morrell in the mail boat and, piloted by Hill the Purser, got into a 'palkie' and was borne up to the office at a good pace by four sturdy natives.

Riding in one of these articles is certainly different to any vehicle in England, more I think approaching the Penny Bus style, only in a palkie one lies down comfortably at full length.

I got to the office and found Mr. Ritchie there and he asked me why I had not come ashore to their house the night before. He said he would put me in harness at once and so, without more ado, I sat down and began to work. There are three others in the office besides myself, Mr. Macaulay, Mr. Turner and Mr. Low, the latter only temporarily, besides about a dozen parsees.

The latter are a curious-looking set of men. They wear just a tight-fitting dressing-gown sort of a coat and shoes which turn up in a point like those you have at home. They have no stockings, and on their head they wear a kind of nondescript affair something between a hat, cap, turban, and roll of tape, if you can fancy such a thing. I hardly know how to describe it, because I do not know how it is made, but it is generally speaking a bright red merino, twisted round so as to fit the head, and then the brim (which is about four inches deep, and varies from about six to eighteen inches width, according to caste) is made by twisting this stuff round and round precisely like a roll of tape. They shave their heads, and in fact wear no hair whatever except a moustache. Their forehead is painted with different devices indicative of their caste, and most of them wear rings in their ears, not where European ladies wear them, but somewhere near the top. They are many of them very intelligent, and speak very good English. They do not all wear these turban affairs as some have great long caps, like a coalscuttle on end, on the top of their heads. These latter do not paint their foreheads; I do not know what is the difference, but probably I shall find out some day.

I drove back with Mr. Ritchie in his brougham and dined with them up at Mazagon where their house is. It is about three miles from the office and one has to drive through the native part of the town which is rather interesting, at any rate to a newcomer.

I suppose there are greater varieties of costume in Bombay than almost anywhere. Many of the natives only wear a string round their waist to which is attached a sort of belly band, like a horse, and which fastens in front and behind. The children, generally speaking, wear nothing at all, except perhaps a ring through their nose, or round their ankles if girls. The women nearly all wear a ring of some sort through their nose. Some of them are very handsome rings set with different sorts of stones, they are nearly all silver, and they also wear silver rings round their ankles, some of them of a prodigious size.

The streets seem always to be swarming with natives who will persist in walking in the middle of the street and getting in the way of all the carriages.

From the office we look over the place where the men were blown away from the guns, which is a large open space supposed to be principally grass, and really as green as Southsea Common sometimes is after a hot summer.[2] We are on the second floor and looking over the sea, so we get nice cool sea breezes the greater part of the day.

We passed through the native streets, which are divided according to the different merchandise sold there. Here you have a row of coppersmiths and there a row of rice or toddy shops and so on. There is a large hospital and a Philanthropic Institution founded by that eminent individual Sir Jamsetjee Jeejeebhoy, Baronet,[3] who has really done an immense amount of good in Bombay, and there is a fine looking Cathedral inside the fort. However, more of these places anon when I have had time to look at them.

Mr. Ritchie has got a magnificent house. It has two storeys, which few bungalows in Bombay have, I think. Downstairs is the dining room, but they do not ever use that. Upstairs they have one immense room running the whole length of the house, which they have screened off into three large rooms which they make dining room, drawing room and a sort of boudoir for Mrs. Ritchie, all large rooms. There are also two bedrooms on that floor built, as it were, on wings, not literally. One Mr. and Mrs. Ritchie's and the other the spare room which Captain Bayley has. I sleep below, next the proper dining room, in a room about the size of the College mess room. I open a door and go out into a sort of passage to cool myself, and then open another door and get into a bath room fitted with all necessaries. I have a bed in the middle of this great room, and it rather puzzled me the first night to get through the mosquito curtains. I let one fellow in, and he paid me out for it, by buzzing about in a disagreeable manner, and now and then kissing one rather hard.

One does not get very much encouraged at first. For instance, I noticed how thin nearly everybody was and, though I knew I was looking rather pale myself, a man was looking at me and saying what a treat it was to see anyone with such a colour.

On Wednesday morning, I drove in with Mr. Ritchie, and in the afternoon went to see *Oriental* off. She is very much altered since we knew her. They have taken a mast out of her and given her two funnels. The old *Oriental* is indeed old, but withal a very fine, comfortable old ship. We do not use her as a regular mail ship now, but only as a troop ship, or for any service of that sort. She is gone up now to bring down a regiment. She was full of passengers going up, half of them children, and nearly all ill. Among the passengers is Lieut. Pim who has had his leg badly hurt in China.[4]

33

Yesterday morning I drove down to the Dockyard with Mr. Ritchie.[5] He went over the *Pottinger* and I went down to the Dockyard office. Captain Robson, our Marine Superintendent, is head there, all of course being under the control of Mr. Ritchie as Commander-in-Chief, as it were. In this office besides Captain Robson there are four, and several parsees.

In the afternoon I went on board the *Pekin* which sailed for China yesterday, with Mr. Ritchie. She is a beautiful vessel and most beautifully kept. I found all the "Electric Telegraph" people, who came down with us, on board. They are ordered round to Madras now, and so will go in the *Pekin* round to Point de Galle, and have to wait there a fortnight for the *Nubia*, unless they send the *Granada* or *Madras* down instead of the poor unfortunate *Ava*.

Capt. Bayley and I dined afterward with Macaulay. I am going to live with him and expect I shall go there on Monday. They have a very nice house indeed, near Mr. Ritchie's, and everything is first rate. The house is not so large and of course not so expensive as Mr. Ritchie's. They have only one large sitting room which is screened off for dining and drawing room. The latter is very elegantly furnished. I think all the furniture is Macaulay's, but Campbell and Whitley live there. I shall make the fourth, and I expect I shall be very comfortable there, as they seem to be very happy and to have everything very nice.

I don't know yet how I shall manage about conveyance. Whitley and Campbell have a nice little shigram and pair between them, and Macaulay has one too, in which I shall most probably come to the office always with him. I shall offer to pay for a share in it, but if (as I have a sort of notion) he wants to keep the shigram as his own, I shall just pay half keep, which won't cost much. Whitley and Campbell are both at the Mazagon office, only ten minutes' drive from the house, while the Fort office, as I said, is three miles away. I expect I shall be very comfortable at "The Rock".[6] I hear they are all regular churchgoers and I know that Macaulay is most particular about Sunday. Mr. and Mrs. Ritchie go to the Scotch Church, which is in the fort, and so they are not able to go more than once a day, generally in the evening.[7]

March 21st

Captain Bayley has got command of the *Sir Jamsetjee Jeejeebhoy* to take her down to Galle to assist at the wreck of the *Ava*, after which, I suppose, he will take up his appointment, but old Twynan does not seem in a hurry to leave, and Capt. Bayley can't go there while he is still here.[8]

I think none of my things seem any the worse for the voyage, but the drinking cup and spoon, etc., are wonderfully tarnished, and one side of my little clock is exactly as if it had been burnt. I have ordered a lot of white things. My trousers will be about 3/- a pair and I am going to have some light Shanghai silk coats made which will be 14/-, waistcoats cost from 3/- to 4/- and so on. I am going to buy a camphor-wood chest of drawers to keep my cloth clothes in and a large press for my white things.

March 22nd

I was at church yesterday evening at Bycullah, about a quarter of a mile from The Rock. It is not unlike an English church, a large square building, but has venetians instead of windows and the punkahs are going all service time, which has an odd appearance. The pews are large and wide and instead of seats, like an English Church, they have armchairs. We had an excellent sermon from the Bishop on the Lord's Prayer. Whitley took me to church with him in his shigram. He is the only churchman in his family, the others all being Dissenters.

I have not yet seen many European ladies, but those I have seen I do not think very much of. Mrs. Ritchie is certainly by far not only the most ladylike but the best-looking I have seen. She is really rather a nice-looking person and I don't think India has done her any harm. The ladies in church appeared to be dressed out 'to the nth' but I did not much like the look of them.

My bedroom is quite open and the birds fly in and out and perch upon the head of my bed and chirp till they wake me, then fly away and crib all sorts of little things out of the room. The other morning a bird flew away with a piece of cotton wool about eight times the size of himself, and I think that they had got a nest in the corner of one of the doors of the room and the cotton wool made a good lining.

My revolver has been much admired by all who understand anything about them. Deane and Adams are not a quarter so well finished, and are much more liable to accidents, as for Tranter's double trigger, I would not carry one in my pocket if anyone would pay me £10; they are always liable to go off unawares, and a fellow very nearly shot himself on board the *Pottinger* with one of them.

March 23rd

I moved up to The Rock last night, having got a servant the first thing Monday morning. He seems a very good servant but unfortunately cannot speak a word of English, and as my knowledge of Hindustani is very limited as yet, we do not get on as well as we might.

The native servants seem to have rather curious notions about toothbrushes. The first day I was at Mr. Ritchie's, two of them came up at different times to say that my room was ready all except a toothbrush, and this morning, when I found that my servant had left my toothbrush, etc., behind, I told him that he must go and fetch it, whereupon he left the room and returned with a couple of old worn out fellows that I should think had been passed round to about fifty natives since their first owner had discarded them.

My servant is supposed to be a good one and so he ought to be, for I have to pay high for him, ten rupees a month or twelve pounds a year. He has some capital characters, so I hope he is a good one, but there is a great scarcity of good personal servants now, as so many officers have been here lately and taken them away. The ordinary wages are seven and eight rupees.

There was a survey of the provisions and accommodation on board the *Pottinger* yesterday, by request of Mr. Ritchie, before all the Military and Naval officers in the place and two or three quartermasters in the Indian Navy. It was great fun to see these latter when the casks of meat were opened (the very ones which were opened at Suez). They said "They'd be blowed if it wasn't a sight better meat than they got themselves", and Col. Wetherall said he only wishes he could get some of the pork for breakfast every morning. The men were actually eating it raw, and then after it was all over they were told that they might each take some on board their ships; they could hardly contain themselves. The result of the survey was just what everyone expected, that they could not possibly have better meat served out to them, and the Committee could not see that there was anything at all for the men to be dissatisfied with, either in the provisions or accommodation.

They say it is very hot in Bombay now, but I have not felt it so hot as I expected I should, though the thermometer is a great deal nearer one hundred than zero. The morning and evening are really beautiful and, from The Rock, the scenery is the most splendid you can imagine. It is very high and so we have a good view for miles around. From the back of the house we look down to Mazagon, the P&O Dockyard and the harbour of Bombay. The other sides, we have a good view of the most beautiful country and the sunset and sunrise are most superb. We have lots of coconut trees about the house, and mango trees and all the Indian trees. The house is not large but very convenient. There is no upstairs at all; all is ground floor.

Captain Robson killed a large cobra in his compound the first night I was at Mr. Ritchie's; he was an immense one, nearly six feet long. They brought him into Mr. Ritchie's but I was fast asleep, so I could not see him for the natives took him away and burnt him under a mango tree before morning, as they have some peculiar notions of very ill luck attending the body of a cobra unless he is burnt. I think the greatest nuisances are the mosquitoes and fleas, both of which abound and both of which are disagreeable. It is amusing to see how mosquitoes will always take to fresh people in preference to old Indians. You will see perhaps a dozen people in a verandah and the mosquitoes swarming round one of them, while they do not touch any of the others.

We are unfortunately out of ice. There has been no ice in Bombay for nearly a month, and everybody has been dying for want of it, but it is expected that we shall have a fresh supply in about a week.

I have seen two or three funerals since I have been here. They anoint the dead man with butter and strew a lot of flowers over him, then carry him away and burn him, making all the time the most hideous row imaginable, beating their tomtoms and dancing and singing more as if they were going to a wedding than a funeral. It is a curious thing that whenever a servant wants a holiday, his mother is sure to die and he has to go to her funeral. One of Mr. Ritchie's servants asked for leave three times in the course of about six or eight months to go to his mother's funeral.

You will have heard by telegraph before this reaches you of Lucknow being entirely in our hands and the ladies saved, troops retiring to the N.W.[9] There is a report that the natives have risen at a place about 300 miles from this and taken some fort, and that troops have been sent down this afternoon to retake it, but I don't know whether there is any truth in it.

The *Singapore* came in this morning from China. They saved nearly all the *Ava's* treasure and mails, and were getting up cargo and baggage as quickly as they could. The ship herself is a complete wreck.

There was an immense tiger killed near here about a fortnight ago by the officers of the *Aden*. Mr. Ritchie has the skin; it stood three feet nine inches high and was four feet round. Such a thing has not been seen in Bombay for twenty or twenty-five years.

We are nearly five hours ahead of you; I often think what you are doing. When I am getting up in the morning, I daresay old Ted is thinking of a cup of tea or a little bit of supper.

May 6th

I am still out at Bhandora with Mr. and Mrs. Ritchie. It is getting very hot in Bombay and it is wonderful how much cooler Bhandora is. We go out and come in every day by the railway, and drive from the station to the office in Mr. Ritchie's brougham and from the Mahlim station to Bhandora (about three miles) in Mr. Ritchie's carriage. The house is on the side of a hill close to the sea and is very cool and pleasant. In the monsoon it would not be a good house to live in as it is only thinly thatched with coconut leaves, and the other night when a thunderstorm came on suddenly and it began to rain, we had the benefit of being drenched through. The view from the top of the hill at Bhandora is the most magnificent prospect anyone can possibly imagine. On one side the sea with a very rocky, barren coast, and on the other a beautiful country with mountains and valleys in the distance, dotted here and there with tents and bungalows.

I find Bhandora, and so does everyone else, to be a sleepy and very thirsty place; the amount of soda-water consumed there is immense. Luckily, soda-water and ice are both very cheap, but Mr. Rodgers manages to make a considerable sum out of the former. We are just off the island of Bombay at Bhandora, and the connection is by means of a very well-built causeway, with a bridge in the middle, a very fine road built at the expense of Sir Jamsetjee Jeejeebhoy.[10] It is not, I believe, generally known in England that this individual made nearly the whole of his almost incredible wealth by dealing in empty bottles!! We have reason to be grateful to him for several roads "built at the joint expense of Government and Sir Jamsetjee Jeejeebhoy", and he has built a Parsee Benevolent Institution, a Parsee Hospital and several schools.

There are a great many people at Bhandora and the place is quite full; some are living in tents on the sea beach. There is a very nice little church there, but there is not a clergyman able to come every Sunday. Last Sunday we had a German there who could not speak English plainly.

The way we spend our day at Bhandora is: about half past five or six, my boy brings a cup of tea and a piece of toast. I get up, rub my eyes, drink the tea and eat the toast, then either go out for a walk or sit in the verandah and write letters. About a quarter past nine, the carriage leaves. The train leaves Mahlim about ten minutes after nine and arrives at Bycullah (where we generally get out) at nine thirty-five. Then we drive to the office, arriving there about ten. Sometimes Mr. Ritchie wants to go to the Dockyard, and then it is eleven or eleven-thirty before we get to office. I don't generally stir out of office (unless it is to go to the tailor's or get an ice at the confectioner's) till a few minutes before five, when we drive off again to Bycullah, catching the train at five twenty-five and getting home in time for a walk before dinner. We generally walk the greater part of the way home. Dinner at seven and go to bed about nine.

I am not at all in love with the generality of unmarried young ladies in India. There are some girls of the name of Tonks (euphonious name, eh!) at Bhandora who are about the most vulgar specimens of "young ladies" I have ever seen. Their father was a Captain in the Indian Navy and their mother is married again to a Mr. Forman, a fat, jolly, goodnatured, vulgar opium inspector with lots of money, and very proud of "Annie" and "Maggy" and beer.

Mangoes are just coming into season. They are considered by most people to be very delicious and the Mazagon mangoes are thought to be the best in India. I think they taste like a mixture of shrimps and furniture polish; perhaps I shall get to like them.[11] I like pumelos pretty well, and dates very much, and we got some fruit called lichees the other day which were very delicious. The grapes too are very good, and they grow pineapples which are nothing special. Water-melons too are nice but, in general, I think the Indian fruits far inferior to our English ones.

Mr. Ritchie is one of the kindest men alive and Mrs. Ritchie is a dear little woman. Mr. Ritchie is a very great man here and has, I suppose, as much influence as anyone in the place. Everybody knows him and everybody whom I have heard speak of him likes him very much. I don't think Captain Robson is a man very well suited to his place and with anyone else but Mr. Ritchie I don't think he would get on at all. He is particularly vulgar and very ignorant and of course very overbearing and imperious. He was never one of the company's Captains but commanded some small merchantman for a short time and got taken into the Dockyard as Dockmaster some years since, from which he has risen to be Marine Superintendent. He seems to be always quarrelling with somebody and I don't think anyone in the service likes him much. I have nothing to do with him in the way of business, and he has always been civil to me, but he is a sort of man who swears before his wife, and walks into Mrs. Ritchie's drawing room with his hat on, etc., etc. His wife, Mrs. Robson, seems a very nice lady-like person and a great deal too good for him. She is a great friend of Mrs. Ritchie's but could hardly enter into the best society here, not but that she is quite fit for it herself, but she has what they call a dash of the tarbrush in her.

Calling hours here are very awkward for people engaged during the day. The time for calling is between eleven and two, during the heat of the day. At two, ladies generally "Tiff" and then go to sleep or lounge about until five or so when they go out for a drive. A lady is scarcely visible after two,

39

indeed it is not etiquette to call unless very familiar.

At Bombay we P&O's have an advantage over everyone in the place in getting provisions, as we can draw all our wine, beer, preserves, etc., and all other articles which come out from home, from the Company's stores at cost price. We also get the use of sheets and pillow cases from the steamers, and all Doctor's expenses paid, but not medicine.

There is a Mr. Knight here, a newspaper proprietor, who is a shade less respectable, if possible, than his namesake at home. His leading articles are nothing but low abuse. He always abuses the P&O and lately, finding that nobody takes any notice, he has taken to personal abuse of Mr. Ritchie, and Mr. Ritchie properly riles him, as the Yankees would say, by not taking the slightest notice of anything he says.

I was so busy on board the *Pottinger* that I don't think I gave you so good an account of the mutiny as I ought. In "The Times" of March 31st there is a good description of it, if you can get that.[12]

I don't quite see what Mr. Paine means that "As the P&O fleet increases, the capability of the captains may diminish, and more losses to be feared. With a small squadron you can pick your men, but expansion has its risks". The examinations to be gone through for the captains are now very strict, much more so than they were a few years ago, and so the captains ought to be better men, and I should think that the larger the fleet, the better the pick there would be among the officers. Taking the average, I believe that the P&O ought to lose about three ships every two years. They have been wonderfully free hitherto till this last year, as the *Great Liverpool, Pacha* and *Douro* were the only vessels lost since the Oriental Line was opened. The *Madrid, Erin* and *Ava* have gone within thirteen months, but the *Ava* is the only one that will be any actual loss to speak of, and there has never been life lost at any of the wrecks.

I have not heard from Alfred since he wrote announcing that dear Mary had been called away It must be a great blow for him, poor fellow, but I hope he may have strength given to him to bear up against it. I know how you will feel it, and how we all do, but I somehow cannot write about it, although I think a great deal. We do not know which of us may be next called away but I pray we may all be as equally prepared to meet our summons as dear Mary was. I did not think when dear Mary went away that it was the last time we should see her on earth. Perhaps you may never any of you see me again. In India, people are alive and well one day, and the next in their graves. As the Lord wills, but if it be His good pleasure, I had very much rather die in England than leave my bones in this far off place. I shall be very

40

glad to have some remembrance of dear Mary, any of her books or whatever she valued and, if Alfred has some of her hair, I should very much like to have a ring made of it. "The Lord gave and the Lord taketh away, Blessed be the name of the Lord." I feel very much for him being left a widower so young; it is a mercy now that the little baby died when it did as, had it outlived its mother, it could not have been well cared for in India with no motherly eye to watch over it.[13]

Please thank Sinclair very much for his last long letter but tell him that it is a great waste not to fill up the paper. He writes on a sheet and a half, and the half sheet is only written upon half of one side, the rest blank.

Mr. Ritchie has announced his intention of giving me a trip to China next winter, as Purser of one of the steamers, to give me an opportunity of seeing a little more of the world, and also a kind of practical insight into the working of the Purser's Accounts on that line. He says he will not send me away yet, because the bad weather is coming on, but if I go in the winter, I shall be nicely set up by the voyage for the next hot weather. It will be quite a combination of business and pleasure, and I like the notion very much.

May 16th

I suppose that you will have heard today the news of dear Mary's having been called away. I know what a blow this will be to you and I trust that God will give you the strength and consolation of His Holy Spirit to comfort you in this affliction.

They are expecting an early monsoon this year and we have had sundry indications that it is approaching. Last night we had a heavy fall of rain, accompanied by thunder and lightning, and the roof let the water in so that there was not a dry spot in the house. We sat at the dinner table under umbrellas, which was rather a novel idea and caused a good deal of amusement. It did not last long however and cleared up the fresher. However, it shows that it won't do to live in a thatched bungalow during the rains and I expect in a week or ten days we shall go back to Goorupdes. Most of the bigwigs, Governor, Bishop, etc., are up at Mahabaleshwar or Matheran, and some of them will stay all the rainy season there. Others make a trip to Ahmednuggur (or, vulgarly, Nuggur) about this time, but most people return to Bombay for the monsoon.

We are getting very short of water and most of the wells supply a doubtful-looking liquid, something of the consistency of pea soup. I have recourse to the sea for my bath and there is some tolerably fair drinking water, but I think I take more sodawater than anything else as other water is not good

41

without sherry or something in it. There is a good deal of beer drunk in Bombay. I find a little at dinner does me good, but I always have it half water or soda water as it is very strong and it does not do to drink much of it. There is no such thing as draught beer in India. It is all bottled and very strong.

I wish some public-spirited man would set up omnibuses in Bombay. I am sure they would pay very well and would do away with a great many of the existing buggies and the impudence of the buggywallahs.

I had a letter from Captain Pullen from Suez by the last mail. He says that, as far as he has as yet seen, he does not anticipate any difficulty in laying down the Electric Cable in the Red Sea. If this is done, and it is hoped it will be before long, we shall have communications with England in a few hours!

I see General Walpole has been making a sad mess of affairs up country and everyone here is very indignant at him.[14] I don't know what they will say about it at home. Last time I was at Alverstoke, everyone was talking about what he had been doing and praising him up to the skies. I am afraid that there is a great deal more to be done yet before these men are quiet, and we shall lose many a brave man and spend many months and a great deal of money before India is tranquil.

The other day when we were at breakfast at The Rock a servant was carrying out a dish and let it fall, and broke it just as he got to the door of the room. "Who did that?" roars out Campbell. No answer (there was not time to make up a lie). "Was it a crow?" "Yes, sir." The man of course didn't get a clout on the head (?). When Mrs. Ritchie was living there, a man once broke half a dozen dishes while washing up and told her that a crow had alighted on the meat safe over his head and dropped a stone into the tub. As a proof of what he said, he produced a stone, which it would take at least twenty or thirty crows to lift.

Crows answer the same purpose here that cats do in England, but a native will never tell the truth if it is possible to tell a lie. They have not the slightest notion of honesty about them, although there is a certain sort of fidelity about most of them which prevents them from robbing their own master. A servant who you might imagine to be perfectly honest and who would never rob you in any way would, nevertheless, rob anyone else to any amount. It is necessary to know something of the value of articles here as a native will nearly always ask three times what things are worth, and sailors and newcomers get very much taken in.

May 18th

I have had the greatest difficulty to get any black-edged paper and cannot get any anywhere with a wide border. I have got a good stock now of narrow-bordered, one sort and another, but I have had to pay about 1/- or 1/3d a quire for it.[15]

I went over the workshops of the Great Indian Railway the other day. They have very fine workshops and machinery and a good stock of all that is wanted. Most of the first- and second-class carriage panels are made of papier mâché, instead of wood, as it does not absorb the heat so much and wears better. A few of the engines have got those curious conical funnels which certainly look very ugly.

Lord Ellenborough's Bill is universally ridiculed in India.[16] I must say that from all I have seen of the Government of India in this Presidency, I think it would be far better to let the present system continue, and not tie everything up with the red tapeism of the Home Government. In doing business with the two governments the difference is wonderful.

At home we have, or had a few months ago, several amounts of thousands of pounds due by the Government for manning the *Himalaya*, etc., etc., and the other services done during the war, which we were unable to obtain from some quibble about "Departments", or something of that sort, and I know that with freight, etc., there was more bother with a paltry Government amount of 10/- or £1 than with a respectable merchant's house there would be for £30,000 or £40,000. No end of vouchers and receipts to be got from all parts of the world and then sent in from one Department to another and back again to the Company, till there was so much paid for postage and stationery as the amount was worth, pretty nearly. Here there is no difficulty of that sort, and if this Government had been so bound up with red tape there would have been nearly all the Europeans in Bombay murdered long before this. Sending the *Madras* away for troops (which came just in time to save Bombay), was all done by private letters between the Governor and Mr. Ritchie, and was settled in the course of a few hours. In England it would have taken at least a fortnight.

We are going to have three new ships out from England in the course of two or three months, the *Malabar*, *Benares* and *Salsette* or *Northam*. I do not think the Calcutta people can complain now, as they have the following large screw steamers on their line which are as fast as any afloat: *Simla*, *Candia*, *Nemesis*, *Alma*, *Nubia*, *Bengal*.

The *Candia* met with an awkward accident the other day when docking. She is an immensely long ship, and the tide was running very strong, and carried her round broadside on the shore, where she lies high and dry and will have to wait till next spring tides before she can be got off.

There was another bit of a row on board the *Oriental*, coming down with troops. The men were like those we had, a set of raw recruits, and the officers mere boys, and they condemned the meat on board. It was surveyed at Aden by the Naval and Military officers there, and pronounced very good. We have regularly got them this time, as all these stores were sent from the Commissariat, and were fresh out from England, but men who had never seen any salt meat opened would always say it is bad, as the best of meat has a most offensive smell to those who are not used to it when first opened, but it is very different to the smell of rotten meat. Mr. Ritchie has determined that he won't let the matter drop till some sort of understanding has been come to, as it is liable to give the P&O a bad name when in reality they are in no fault at all. My own opinion is that the fault is not so much with the men, for most of them know no better, being probably fresh from a field or a factory, but with the officers for giving in to them.

On board the *Madras* on her last voyage, some of the men came aft to the officer in command, and complained of various things the first day. The officer was an old hand and said "Is there anything else you have to complain of?" "No, sir." "Then right about face, quick march" and the men were as comfortable as could be the whole voyage. In the *Oriental*, fifty or sixty of the men broke into the spirit room, ran off with about 300 bottles of beer, wine and spirits, and then got drunk and challenged any men in the ship to fight, and so on.

All this makes it very unpleasant for our officers; on the Southampton side they could easily put a few in irons, but here with only a Lascar crew this cannot be done, for any one of them would walk through five or six Lascars. That is the great reason why they wait till they get to Suez for complaints for, as the men on the *Pottinger* said, "Who's to stop us?" However, till after the monsoon there will be no more troops brought overland, and by the time they begin again it is to be hoped they will be able to make some arrangements to keep them in order.

May 19th

I am beginning to like mangoes and eat three or four a day. They are a luscious fruit, yellow sort of pulp inside which is scooped out with a spoon, and a huge stone.

I have been troubled a good deal with prickly heat, which is a sort of rash that comes out all over the body and smarts very much on taking off one's clothes and on going into one's bath. They say it is a sign of good health, so I must not grumble at it.

May 31st

We have a Captain Weston staying with us now. He is Captain of the *Oriental*, and is I think the best amateur performer I ever heard. He has also a very good voice, and he will sit down to his harmonium and play and sing a whole oratorio through without any music; the only thing is we sometimes get a little too much of a good thing, and he sits playing till two o'clock in the morning. He plays all sorts of sacred music most beautifully, and his instrument is certainly a beautiful one. As I write, the "Hallelujah Chorus" is sounding in my ears and, though it wants a chorus to do it justice, it is nevertheless very beautiful. When speaking he has an impediment in his speech, and recommends sea-water bathing because it is a good t—t—onic. He has a beard down considerably below his waist which, when dressed, he tucks in under his clothes, so that he does not appear to have a particularly long one, but when we come to the light and airy style, which we do morning and evening, his immense beard appears to full advantage. Occasionally he will pull it out and astonish people who have never seen it before, particularly ladies.

I suppose you will have been expecting a description of my fellow inmates of "The Rock". To begin with Macaulay. He is a little man, standing about my height, and slim, what you would call a pretty little man and, of course, a great dandy. I like him very much indeed, but he is peculiar, and I think not very good tempered, especially when he thinks his dignity is called in question. He is, moreover, a great Radical and won't drink the Queen's health, has curious absurd ideas about republics and popular government, and knocks "Church and State" on the head, so we don't agree at all in politics; in fact Capt. Bayley who is the greatest Radical I had ever met before, yields the palm to him. Nevertheless, he is a very nice fellow and I think is very much liked everywhere.

Campbell is a good-natured, jolly redfaced man, fond of good eating and drinking, and always full of jokes and anecdotes, not very refined but always polite in the extreme to ladies. I think Whitely is more improved than anyone I know. As we are all provided with firearms, he finds such an old-fashioned weapon as a long bow is no use. He is very well informed and clever; his principal habit is the Cockney failing of frequently dropping his h's, which doesn't sound well, and I hope I may be able to tease him out of it. Altogether we are a very comfortable party without any disagreeables at all, and I think I may consider myself very fortunate in being so comfortably situated.

The Governor gave a Grand Ball on the Queen's Birthday at Matheran.

45

Of course, I did not go, nor did any of our people as they did not think it worthwhile to go eighty miles for a ball. I have not yet been to Government House; I meant to have gone there to breakfast one morning but the news of dear Mary's death came just at the time.

Before coming into a room, the servants always leave their shoes outside. Mrs. Ritchie's little dog is very fond of bringing them into the room and hiding them somewhere, and the men get so savage with him. When Mr. Ritchie was living at The Rock, he had a cockatoo which used to watch his opportunity and steal the men's shoes and carry them down to the bottom of the hill and hide them under the bushes or somewhere.

I see that Yeh (pronounced Yep) is a prisoner in Calcutta.[17] He does not call himself a prisoner but says he has gone down there to have some private conversation with the Queen of England about the doings at Canton.

The Monsoon has now set in, though as yet but mildly, and the rain though heavy is not as incessant as it will be. The number of insects about is something wonderful and the size of them so very much larger than one sees in England. For instance, the other day I caught a spider as big round as an ordinary tea saucer when the legs were out, and we have great winged ants as long as my little finger. We killed a snake last night, not a very large one, but nevertheless an ugly customer to have trodden upon as it was one of a very deadly kind. He measured about three feet from end to end.

I have had an old schoolfellow staying with me the last two days, a boy who used to clean my boots and so on at school, Tomlinson by name. He was in the Mathematical School and is on board one of the merchantmen in the harbour. I should have got on with my letters much better if it had not been for him, for he is such a tremendous chatterbox that there is no doing anything while he is near.

I think that if I keep my eyes open I shall learn more business in a year in Bombay than in six or seven years in London. There is no lack of work here, and it is of a more general kind than in London, not sticking to one particular department.

I don't know if I told you the system of marriage they have here at the Bycullah School. This, you must know, is a sort of National School. These children are looked upon in a manner as public property. They are all orphans or foundlings, mostly half-castes, but when a man wants a wife from there, he goes to the schoolmistress and gets invited to tea. At tea, about a dozen of the eldest girls are present and he takes his choice and tells the schoolmistress who he has chosen. There is then an enquiry made into his character and, if they see no cause or impediment, the pair are married.

In this way, dozens of marriages are contracted every year in Bombay, and by the most respectable people. I do not by any means mean to say that I ever intend to follow out this plan. Oh No! I promise you that if I ever should get married in this country, my wife comes out from England to me. I do not at all approve of country-born girls, more especially half-castes.

Our dinner table presents rather a curious appearance at this season. Almost directly the table is laid, a whole lot of winged ants make their appearance on it. Each of them has four wings which he sheds and then crawls away like a maggot and dies. By the time the dinner is over, the table is covered with wings. There are frequently a number of black ants who come and fight with these winged fellows and then the scene is most ludicrous. It would, however, be perfectly useless for me to attempt to describe all the insects I come across as they are so numerous. I am making a collection for Croker, who is a member of the Entomological Society, but do not get on very well; not that I have not got some very curious specimens, but I find that the servants always get hold of them and throw them away which is most provoking, particularly as some I had got were very rare and not often or easily obtained.

June 4th

The steamer is to be detained till daylight tomorrow morning for important Government despatches. What they are, we have yet to learn, but I expect it is only that the Governor is lazy and won't finish his letters in time for the midday post today.

June 18th

We were sitting out on the verandah one evening after dinner, when Macaulay was suddenly taken in a choking fit and went in and lay down on the sofa, when he went off into hysterics, throwing himself about and calling out for Mr. Ritchie. First of all whispering and then calling out much louder than he possibly could had he been all well, "Where's Mr. Ritchie? Is he dead? Ah, who says he's dead? Who dares to say it? It is a lie!", etc. He would go on like this till he exhausted himself and then would begin again. This lasted for about two hours, when the Doctor came, also Mr. Ritchie and Captain Robson, the latter only hoping the mail would be in and then going away. We got mustard poultices on to him and at last put him to bed.

Worthington was with us at the time and was a great help, but made us leave off and burst out laughing now and then. For instance, when they were wiping away the mustard from his (Macaulay's) chest, Worthington said confidentially that he was making a clean breast of it, which sent everybody laughing out of the room. He has been staying near us for some little time past, studying Hindustani, and so we see a good deal of him of an evening. He would persist in sitting up all night with Macaulay. We none of us turned in till nearly two, and I thought I would relieve him, so I got up again soon after three and sat out in the verandah outside Macaulay's door so that I might hear if anything went wrong. Macaulay went away in the *Pottinger* for a change of air to China on Wednesday.

June 19th

The drainage here is most execrable and I really wonder that any Europeans can live in the stinks that we get sometimes. The other day it was exactly like being in the middle of a large sewer, the smell enough to knock one down all over the island, but at Mazagon particularly. In some parts of the native town, there is a quantity of beautiful black stagnant water which stinks most abominably, but the natives are too lazy to clear it away, and yet there are people who profess to look after these things. I think the Commissioners of Sewers must take in needlework, or else they squabble with one another "how not to do it", so that whatever it is they are quarrelling about, of course, remains undone.

There was a report in the bazaar, two days ago, that one of Lindsay's ships had gone down with all hands and a large cargo. It however turned out a hoax. These kind of hoaxes are very common, I suppose to funk the native underwriters; nearly all our ships have been lost over and over again, and the cry of "wolf" is so frequent that when a wolf comes, the case of the *Erin's* wreck for instance, it takes a long time to make them believe it. Oh! these natives are a horrid set; the more I know of them, the more I detest them, and those who know them most like them least.

June 26th

You will have Alfred with you ere this, and I hope he will have been of some comfort to you. I wish I might have been at home at this time to have been with you, but that could not be, and it makes me all the more anxious to hear how you have borne it.

The last day or two I have changed my thin black alpaca trousers for the thick dark ones I was wearing last winter at home, and have not felt too hot. I have also had drawers on, which I did not wear before. How damp everything feels and is, to be sure. Pyjamas and nightshirt feel quite moist when one puts them on in the evening, and other clothes ditto in the morning. One is glad to sleep under a blanket, though it is not cold, but so intensely moist (damp hardly expresses the feeling), the moisture creeping in everywhere. I find my razors, which are beautifully polished with washleather by my boy one morning, the next all spotted with rust. The binding of books gets spotted. As for my revolver, he requires constant looking after every day to keep him in anything like decent order. My boots get mouldy, my clothes ditto, and my toothbrush always has a fine coating of mould every morning which I have to wipe off and use as one cannot afford a new toothbrush each morning. I find the weather very depressing; I don't enjoy my bath, my breakfast, my dinner or, in fact, anything of any sort and feel quite spent when my day's work is over. However, I must not grumble for I think everybody is the same, more or less, and I daresay it will soon go off.

I do not find people write to me nearly as much as I had hoped they would. Altogether, I have received from England nineteen letters while, including those I wrote by this mail, I have sent sixty-one.

June 30th

The last mail brought news from England of old Commodore Brook's death.[18] Poor old man. I do not think it was unexpected by anybody as he had looked for years as though he would pop off suddenly some day. During the last two or three years of his life he has never missed his two bottles of brandy a day. His son, who is up in China, was married the other day, just about the same time that his old father died.

I see Captain Townsend is going to bring out a small new steamer for the Company, under canvas to Bombay. Is his wife coming with him, I wonder? I should think if she does that she will have enough of the sea by the time she arrives at Bombay, sailing out in a small vessel the size of a gunboat.[19]

You will see that Mr. Willcox is elected Chairman of the P&O.[20] As I was not able to see him before I came away, I wrote to him some time since, thanking him for all his kindness to me.

They have one or two days been expecting a row in Bombay and I believe some kind of conspiracy has been found among the natives. The day the last mail left, everyone was prepared and sailors have since then kept guard in the Fort at night. Mrs. Matthey asked Capt. Weston and me to dinner with her that night and bring our pistols with us. However, nothing happened, but the native feasts are coming on and we may probably have some little disturbance, though I do not think there is anything to be frightened of.

49

A shocking accident happened here the other day; as a ship was going out of harbour a sea struck her and damaged the ship very much, broke both the Captain's legs, and upset the pilot boat, sending the pilot and thirteen natives into the water, and drowning them all.

Worthington is frequently up here but I am afraid we shall soon lose him, as his examination comes off on Monday. He and Weston are great friends. Really I think Weston is the best fellow I have met for a long time. He has a hobby (which most men have). His is against shaving, and he has written a book about it, bringing forward all sorts of proofs from Scripture and History to shew that men were intended to wear their beards. His own reaches down to his waist, and he tucks it in under all his clothes when he is dressed, and you would think to look at him that he had cut it short. He is very well-connected and is a bit of a scholar, can read the Greek Testament, knows something of Latin, French and Italian, and almost everything else, and speaks Hindustani like a native. Altogether he is a most agreeable fellow and I shall be very sorry when he goes.

I think most probably the old *Oriental* will be here the whole of the monsoon through. She is too slow for a mail ship, but what a splendid old ship she is. I went to see her in dry dock. All the scientific men of the place came down to look at her, and there were dozens of Indian Naval officers always around her. White put her bow on her, and I believe it is his favourite. The old ship has done her work uncommonly well and has been a very faithful servant to the Company.

The police regulations in Bombay are very good, though the policemen are a poor, skinny-legged set. Mr. Forsitt, the Inspector, is the man who dressed himself in a native's clothes and attended a meeting, when it was proposed to murder all the principal men here, and they were rather astounded to find themselves under arrest next morning.

Whenever I take a buggy, I always make it a rule to give the man his fare and no more, as the buggywallahs are very impudent and always expect double fare, in fact, are never contented if you give them double, they want quadruple and so on. Well, when I reached the bungalow, I tendered the man his fare which he refused, whereupon I told him that he should not have a piece more and went inside the house to get the printed list to show him. When I was gone he began abusing Weston who was sitting outside, and told him that if he or I ever came down to the Bunder wanting a buggy, we shouldn't get one if he could help it as he would tell all the other buggywallahs that we never gave them "chevymerry". This was too much for Weston's weak nerves and, seizing the fellow's whip, he gave him three or four pretty smart blows across the back, whereat the fellow yelled lustily and set his horse galloping down the hill, turning round and abusing us in a whiny crying schoolboy kind of tone directly he thought he was out of reach. He had not been gone ten minutes before I found I had lost my pocket book. It contained nothing valuable, but all the letters I had received by last mail, and other papers of no value to any but the owner but which I was very much put out at losing as I thought the buggywallah would be sure not to give it back after his licking, and I could not prove that he had got it. However, he came up during the evening and privately informed my servant that he had got the pocketbook but was not going to give it up after the licking he had had. He did not think I had remembered to take his number. The next day, I wrote to the Inspector detailing the circumstances and, half an hour afterwards, he sent my pocketbook up.

It is generally found that the so-called Christianized natives are really some of the worst of them and only allow themselves to be baptised because they think that they will be more trusted by their masters and have more opportunities of robbing them than before. They are generally men who have lost caste and will not be received by their friends, so they adopt that as a last resource. From all I can see and hear in Bombay, at least, the efforts of stated missionaries avail very little towards Christianizing the natives, but there is no doubt that Christianity has a kind of insensible influence over the people generally which must lead to good eventually.

July 3rd

Today would have been poor dear Mary's birthday. I hope and trust she is far happier than she would have been had she lived. A day like this brings her memory more forcibly before one than usual, though there is rarely a time that I am not thinking of her.

February 7th, 1859 [21]

It is, as you say, very curious that the fomenters of all the disturbances at Portsmouth should all be called away in so sudden a manner.[22]

I breakfasted at Government House the other morning. Mr. Davis and I went together. It was rather slow, but I think is proper to be done, if only for once, as it gives one the entrée into Government House. I sat directly opposite to Lord Elphinstone and could not help noticing the marvellous likeness between him and Mr. Ritchie which one notices even more when close than at a distance.

The way one manages is this. The day before one sends a pasteboard in to the A.D.C.-in-waiting at the Town Major's office with "Breakfast tomorrow" on it (there are two public breakfast days a week) and then at half past nine o'clock one drives up to the door of Puell House, where are ranged any number of puckah sepoys in flaring red coats, drawn up in line to greet the visitors as they come in. Then one walks up a large flight of stairs into an ante-room and writes one's name down in a book, then after waiting some quarter of an hour or so talking, etc., in comes Lord Elphinstone and each person is introduced to him, then down we go to breakfast, a very good breakfast, but nothing very particular. I had however some of the finest poached eggs I ever tasted, and some Mahabaleshio, a peach which seemed to call up a slight remembrance of Cornwall.

I have today an invitation from his Lordship to go up and dine there tomorrow evening to meet Mr. Woodcock who has come down from Ahmednuggur and is going home by the mail. It is rather a nuisance the night before the mail leaves, and I am afraid that your letter will be cut short in consequence, but I did not think it right to decline the invitation, especially as I am not likely to have another opportunity of seeing Mr. Woodcock.

Last Saturday, Mr. George Whitley was united to Miss Grace West at Bycullah Church. I was asked to the breakfast, and put off mourning for the day, and not having a decent pair of trousers to go in, invested in a tremendous pair of shepherd's plaid pegtops which, bye the bye, I made to do duty for the Governor's Breakfast beforehand. I chose them because I could wear them at all times, in or out of mourning, and they are beautiful stuff which I hope will last me a very long time. And so they ought you will say when you hear the price I had to pay for them, Rs21 & £2.2.0. Fancy that for a pair of trousers alone! I also had lavender kid gloves for the same reason, as I thought it a pity to throw away Rs12 on a pair of white ones which I could only wear once as they can't clean gloves here. I made my old blue frock coat do, and wonderfully well it looked, and what with a swell white waistcoat and Mr. Maul's blue and gold tie, I think I did very well especially as I had some gold wriststuds.

There were three bridesmaids and there was to have been a fourth but, through some oversight, she was not asked until it was too late. Macaulay was best man and two of the bride's brothers the two groomsmen. The bride looked beautiful; she is certainly a sweet girl in every way, and he may look upon himself as a most fortunate man. Mrs. Townsend and Mrs. Ponsonby were the married ladies to take charge of the bridesmaids and I took it upon myself to superintend the lady visitors up in the gallery and keep them in order. The service was very nicely conducted, the only misfortune being the unfortunate native who was blowing the bellows of the organ would keep looking round the corner every minute or so to see what was going on, upon which the organ would give a kind of convulsive gasp and suddenly stop, upon which he would of course begin puffing away more lustily than ever.

After the wedding was over, we went to Mr. Ritchie's where a splendid breakfast had been provided, and sat down a party of between twenty-five and thirty. There was the usual amount of speechifying, and I was originally put down as having to return thanks for the bridesmaids, but the programme altered and though I had prepared no end of a speech, it went for nothing. I was then congratulating myself that I had nothing to do but when it came to the last toast but one, 'The Ladies', Dan Turner, who had to return thanks, looked across the table and called out to me to do it, turning very red and looking very much to be pitied.

Mr. Lock, the Company's travelling Inspector, arrived the day before the wedding, and I suppose will be here about a fortnight. He seems an extremely clever, well-informed and thorough man of business. He was, I think, an Eton boy and is extremely well up in everything.

They have just started a P&O club here which, if well managed, is I think likely to be a very good thing. It has answered uncommonly well in Calcutta, and I think will be well supported here. I, in common with the other shore employees, have paid an entrance fee, but we are not to be charged a monthly subscription as all the officers afloat, who avail themselves of it, will be. It may be very handy sometimes if one wants to ask a friend to dinner, or give him a bed, when from any reasons it could not be so well done at the bungalow.

February 9th

I must not forget that today is your birthday and most heartily do I pray that every blessing may be showered down upon you from Him who is the author of all good.

I spent a very pleasant evening last night at the Bishop's. Mr. Woodcock I like very much; his manner is rather offhand but that wears off.

February 23rd

Here's a piece of news that will, I think, rather astonish you a little. Next month about this time I hope to be, not at home, but half way there, and then I'm going down to Australia! The fact is this: I have an offer of a trip in the *Benares* at which I have jumped at once, and she is to leave on the twelfth of next month and go up to Suez, from thence to The Mauritius and then to Australia, returning to Suez and back to Bombay.

I think the trip will do me a great deal of good and will enable me to see something more of the world, etc. I shall get a practical insight into the workings of the Purser's Department, of which at present I know very little about, shall see something more of the world, have a little knocking about, though I hope a very pleasant voyage, shake up my liver a bit and, last of all, perhaps save a little money, but I am doubtful on this latter head. There are other disadvantages to be placed in the opposite scale: the leaving a comfortable shore billet for all the annoyances and discomforts of a sea life, the expense of clothes, the possibility of being thrown with disagreeable officers, and having to endure the growls of discontented and sea-sick passengers, etc., etc.

I went to the Governor's Ball but did not dance at all. I stood up for one quadrille but had to sit down again as we were a couple too many. However, it was a very pretty sight and I would not have missed it for something. There were lots of people I knew there and I might have danced all the evening if I had been able. One young lady is reported to be very jealous because I did not ask her to dance. What do you think of that? There have been all sorts of balls and parties in Bombay lately, but I have not been able to go to any of them. There was a large ball given some time ago at a native's house, in farewell to the Manager of one of the Banks who has gone home, and all the great people were invited. The Bishop was saying that he had an invitation for it addressed to "Mr. & Mrs. Lord Bishop", which he intended to keep as a curiosity.

The *Cyclops* arrived in Bombay the other day. I have not seen Captain Pullen yet but instead intend calling upon him tomorrow after the mail leaves.

On Monday we had a piece of news which gladdened the heart of more than one person in Bombay, viz., a telegram to say that the *Mazagon* arrived safely at Cochin on the 26th and so will be here in about ten days. This is a great relief, for many people had begun to think that she had made a hole in the water. She will have been eight months over by the time she arrives.

The P&O Club was opened on Tuesday, with a large farewell dinner to Macaulay. The Club is really a first-rate place, and is likely to be an immense convenience to officers afloat. The dinner went off very well, with the usual amount of toasts and speeches, and was, I think, a very nice thing, and it showed the good feeling that exists towards Macaulay.

Mr. Lock, our Inspector, is still here but will, I believe, leave for China by the next mail. He is a vastly superior man to most P&O's and is in fact a thoroughly well-educated man in every way. He has brought some first-rate introductions to Bombay and has been living at Government House for the last ten days with Lord Elphinstone.

NOTES

1. Mr. Ritchie was the P&O Agent in Bombay.

2. The Indian Mutiny only affected the fringes of Bombay, and although there are numerous instances recorded of the execution of Sepoys in Bengal by "blowing away from the guns" during the early days of the Mutiny, I can find no reference to such events in Bombay.

3. Born in 1783, a Parsee, and orphaned at an early age, Sir Jamsetjee Jeejeebhoy made his way through life unaided. By the time of his death in 1859 he had founded many charitable institutions including schools, homes and hospitals, etc. He was knighted in 1842 and made a baronet in 1858 in recognition of his charitable works.

4. Kendall was named after the explorer Franklin (possibly an Uncle). Lt. Pim served on one of the Franklin search expeditions in 1853.

5. The Mazagon Docks were built by P&O in the 1860's and remained in P&O Group ownership until 1961.

6. The Rock was the name of Macaulay's house. The sharing of houses, or "chummeries", by young Assistants was an economical and common practice in the East.

7. St. Andrew's and St. Columba's of the Church of Scotland.

8. A 125-ton paddler, *Sir Jamsetjee Jeejeebhoy* was named after the Indian philanthropist.

9. Following the massacre of women and children in Cawnpore, news of the fate of those defending Lucknow was anxiously awaited. The news, when it came, was received by a wave of public relief.

10. This causeway still links Bombay with Bandra (modern spelling).

11. He does. See his entries for May 19, 1858 and May 12, 1861.

12. See illustration.

13. Mary was Kendall's married sister and was living in Calcutta at the time of her death. Her husband, Alfred Martell, may have been in the Indian Civil Service. Refer also to Kendall's entry for November 18th, 1859.

14. Following the capture of Lucknow, Lieutenant-General Walpole attacked Fort Ruiya and was repulsed with heavy losses, for which he was subsequently severely censured.

15. Kendall was in mourning for his sister Mary. The width of the black edging indicated the closeness of a person to the deceased.

16. Lord Ellenborough was at this time President of the Board of Control. There he drafted a new scheme for the government of India, a change considered essential after the Mutiny.

17. At Canton, the Viceroy Yeh hauled down the British flag flown from a Hong Kong-registered ship and thus provoked retaliatory action. Lord Elgin took Canton in 1857 and took Yeh captive.

18. Commodore Brook is thought to have been a former naval colleague of Edward Kendall. He must have had quite a constitution to have handled two bottles of brandy a day!

19. The *Mazagon* was a small 86-ton paddle steamer, built for P&O in 1858 for service in Bombay harbour. It was impractical to steam her to India from Britain, so she was sailed all

the way, an extremely hazardous journey in such a small craft unfitted for use as a sailing ship. Captain Townsend's wife was undertaking an extremely perilous journey and it is surprising that P&O allowed this.

20. Brodie McGhie Willcox was one of the founders of the P&O Company who had retired as a Managing Director in 1854. He continued to serve as a Director until he was appointed Chairman in 1858, a post which he held until his death in 1862 when Arthur Anderson succeeded him.

21. There is here a gap of six months in the letters.

22. This may be a reference to two meetings held in December 1858 protesting against the suspension of the curate of St John's, Portsea, who was suspended, and later sacked, for appearing intoxicated at an annual Sunday School teachers' party. His defence was that he had been prescribed brandy for a stomach ailment and, when this had no effect, had taken sal volatile as well.

4 Picking up a man overboard from the Candia in the Red Sea in 1861

5

On Board "Benares" and "Oneida"

March 21st, 1859, on board *Benares*

I have not had anything like a letter from Sinclair for an age, so that I don't
know any particulars about the dog you mention, further than that in one of
his last notes, he said that he was not able to write a long letter because a dog
had followed him home the night before, the precise meaning of which I was
at a loss to define.

The *Mazagon* arrived at Bombay in tow of the *Pekin*, two days before we
left. She was reported at Cochin all well on the 20th February. There was
an absurd cock and bull story in the Bombay paper about her having been
abandoned at sea, etc., an exaggerated report, of course, of the Chief Officer
having been sent away in a boat to Cochin to report her. I am glad that I saw
Capt. Townsend before I came away. The *Mazagon* looks like a largish
ship's boat alongside one of our larger steamers, and the only wonder on
looking at her and the way she is rigged, etc., is not that she was eight months
coming out, but that she ever fetched Bombay at all. Capt. Townsend
reports very favourably of her as a sea-boat but says she won't sail at all. She
looks very little larger than the *Bee*.[1]

If Edward and Sinclair are both at home in the summer, I think they might
get a trip to Alexandria and come across to meet me at Suez when the
Benares goes up again. Wouldn't that be jolly?

I am sure you can hardly fancy me in gold lace and brass buttons! I found
that it would be better for me to have my name on the ship's books on
account of drawing the pay from the ship and not from the office while
away, and so, being an officer of the ship, I am obliged to wear a uniform
on muster days and Sundays, though I need not do it at other times. I must
say that I have rather an objection to wearing it, except when necessary, but
it does not much matter.

I did not think it worth while to buy any as I am not likely to go for more
than the one, or at most two, trips, so I came out in borrowed plumes, having
a coat of Davies's, and a gold band of Marshall's. He happened to have a
new one covered in crêpe which had been given him by a Naval officer in
China, and so it just does. I had a pair of blue cloth trousers built for me,
but I shall also make them do, for what I very much want is a new pair of

evening dress trousers as my old ones are beginning to be the worse for wear.[2]

This ship has as fine accommodation for passengers as any ship afloat, I should think. She is nine feet high between decks, but has one or two disadvantages. She has magnificently large ports, but they are so near the water that she can't keep them open when there is the least sea on, especially as from her peculiar model, she reels very heavily. She is a magnificent ship in fine weather but I don't know what she will be in a gale or wind. I never was in any ship where there was so little vibration from the screw; except just over the propeller, one can hardly feel it at all, and in the fore part of the ship you would not think she was under way when she is not rolling. I am writing this quite in the after part of the saloon and, though not without the feel of the screw underneath, there is less motion from it than either in the *Ripon* or *Pottinger* from the paddles, and they generally find a screw ship the worst. This ship has a Griffith's screw, and I daresay there is a great deal in that.

The Captain (Skottowe) has more polish about him than many P&O Captains, and is a very religious man and a good man of business. The Chief Officer is a very clever and gentlemanly man; he was one of the senior Captains in Green's Service, and has only just entered the P&O. His name is Parish and he is rather a celebrated man in his way, having written one or two books on maritime affairs. The Purser is one of the best men I ever came across, and the Doctor is another very good fellow, so that I daresay I shall do very well. Of the other officers, I can't say very much. The Third seems an agreeable enough fellow, and so is the Second, but he is a very rough specimen, a man of no education whatever, and not particularly bright I think. There are, besides two others, a Fourth and Supernumerary Fifth. The ship steams very well but I don't think she quite comes up to what was expected of her on that point.

I hear everywhere that Parliament is likely to be dissolved shortly. I suppose the Squire will be standing again for Cornwall?[3]

Europe seems in a very ticklish position just now and surely France will not keep clear much longer.[4] I only hope that England may keep out of it, though I am afraid she will think that she must have a finger in the pie somehow. What a terrible thing a war with France would be just now. Setting aside every other consideration, what would India do? Where would the Indian mails go and what would become of the P&O? It would be rather awkward if, on steaming into The Mauritius on our return from Australia, we were to find ourselves laid hold upon as a prize and, as we should have but little coal in the bunkers, we could not shew them our heels to any great advantage.

A sea life is to me monotonous after one has once got into the way of it, that there is very little of interest to write about. We expect to get to Suez tomorrow night or early on Saturday morning (26th), and shall probably leave again on the following day. This will not give much rest but we took in coal enough at Aden to last us back again so that there will be not much to do.

We have some very nice people among the passengers, but too many "blessed babbies" to make it quite like paradise. Sir John Lawrence is a passenger on board, but has been very sea-sick all the way and has not shewn up much.[5]

There is an amusing character who sits next to me at table, Sir John Lawrence's secretary, who knows what the good things of this life are as well as anyone, and who takes his bottle of claret at breakfast and another, sometimes more, at dinner regularly. He also manages generally to dine off six or seven different dishes and enjoys his cheroot afterwards as much as anybody. The other day the ship was rolling a great deal and there was a very thin attendance at dinner. I was carving a leg of boiled mutton (which he generally begins with) and asked him to take some. "No, thanks", said he, "I don't feel equal to it today, in fact I don't think I shall be able to eat anything, I feel very poorly." However, "Steward, just bring me a little of that beef steak pudding." He had a large helping of that, which he managed to put away very quickly, and found it had given him an appetite, he said, so he had the leg of turkey and afterwards some fowl and ham, finishing up with a huge plateful of curry and rice, and when the pastry came on table, eating fruit tart, plum pudding, custards and I don't know. I said to him, "I don't think you've done too badly for a sick man." "Well, I don't know, I haven't made half a dinner today." I said to myself, well, I'd sooner keep you for a week than a fortnight, if I had the paying for your mess.

March 26th

We arrived at Suez before daylight, and waited till after breakfast, when the small steamer came alongside for the passengers. On shore they went, and the Purser and I went with them. There is generally a bit of a sea on at Suez and the little steamer was tossing about in fine style, so that Sir John Lawrence, while listening to the salute which the *Pelonis* was giving, had to lie down on the deck as sick as he could be.

By the way, the *Benares* has been saluted with 17 guns on leaving each port, whether in honour of Sir J.L. or Mr. F.R.K. we won't say.

We got on shore and had some tiffin at the Hotel, and then it was found that one of the passengers, Col. Russell, had left all his baggage on the ship, having given orders to the steward not to move it till he came on board again, and all the time he intended going on to Cairo. This was very provoking, but there was no help for it and so I volunteered to go off to the ship again, which I did, but as the way is rather roundabout, I did not get back again till nearly five o'clock. This had delayed the train some time, but at last they got off satisfactorily enough.

I saw Mr. Anderson, but did not have the opportunity of speaking to him, as he was busy with Sir John Lawrence at the time and went away to Cairo the next morning.[6]

From the position of Suez one has to make a long round to go on shore or on board, as there is a large shoal extending for some distance out over which no boat can pass. This is very inconvenient and very often makes the nearest ship to the town the farthest off, as far as getting on shore is concerned. It was blowing a fresh wind and dead against us, so we were as you may imagine a long time getting out, and having scarcely tasted anything since breakfast (for we were all too busy to get much tiffin), we were tolerably hungry, and our Arab friend took us across the end of the spit, where, although we did not stick, we were perpetually going bump, bump, every instant dousing us all and not improving the linen. However, we got past that and after sundry long tacks fetched just under the stern of the *Candia*, when oh! such a smell of dinner going on assailed us, such a clatter of knives and forks and smell of good things, that we poor hungry mortals were very wet, not only outside our clothes, but inside our mouths.

After a good many ineffectual attempts we reached the *Benares*, and, as there was a heavy sea on, had to fend off the boat from the side, which Mr. Slaughter did with the tiller. He, the Purser and Chief Steward then managed to jump on to the ladder, and I was next on the list, being on the thwart ready for my opportunity, when at a more than ordinary pull the painter gave way and away he went, having left two of our Arab crew on the ladder. I made the other two get up sail, when lo and behold there was no tiller, the Admiralty Agent having either taken it on board with him or dropped it overboard. I managed to fit in a bit of plank which we luckily found in the bottom of the boat and then we went on a cruise again, I taking the helm. We were obliged to make one or two long tacks about before we could pick up the ship again, and then got the other side, which was luckily to leeward, but we found there was no ladder. What was to be done? One man proposed getting into a port, which would be all very well if there were no bar across and one could once get well in; at last after about ten minutes waiting I spied a kind of port gangway made for hoisting in light packages, etc., but in reach when the boat rose. I clutched hold of this and after one or two ineffectual attempts slung myself on to it, and then it was easy to get on board.

The others followed my example and, except one who tumbled back upon the linen and didn't hurt himself, we got on board all right, in time to sit down to some dinner about half past nine instead of being on board by a little after five. We, of course, got nicely laughed at for this by the Admiralty Agent, and Purser more especially, though we were not much more than half an hour after them, but I can tell you I was not sorry to get on board.

March 27th

Coaling ship, dirty mess. After morning service, went on board the *Madras* and spent the day with my old friends there.

No sign of *Salsette*. All the *Madras* men very sorry as they will have to go down to Bombay, except poor Barron, the Purser, newly married and wife at Bombay, who hopes to goodness the *Salsette* won't make her appearance. Everybody else hopes she will, both for the credit of the Company and their own comfort, as they want another fortnight in the beautiful cold air of Suez. Spent a very pleasant evening and returned on board about ten.

March 28th,

5 a.m. Look out of my cabin door, see officer of the watch just coming below. "*Salsette* in?" "I believe you she is, came in at midnight." Hurrah, the first mail under the new contract is in time, which it never has been under any other. Bravo! We learn that she would have been up earlier but that she encountered a fearful gale off Mauritius and was obliged to be hove to for nearly a whole day. A hundred and four passengers, all landed about nine and not a vestige of them on going on shore at eleven.

Meet Capt. Methven, the new-appointed Commander of the *Salsette*, and ask him if he will be ready to take down the Bombay mail.[7] "Oh, yes, have the ship ready in six hours, if they'll only give me the coal, and I don't want much." (Very well, that's all right.) Get the passenger list, go on board, have dinner and help the Purser to arrange the berthing of the passengers by the time they come on board.[8]

6 p.m. Passengers begin to arrive in dribble, steamer comes alongside at seven with all that have not arrived before, baggage, mails, etc., etc. Then all excitement, bustle, growling, grumbling, dissatisfaction, discomfort, looking for luggage, missing something, finding it, one man abusing the P&O because they don't put his luggage on top, another slipping into the Transit Administration for damaging a bandbox, etc., etc., an old fat strong-minded French lady with spectacles on, pointing with her parasol at every canvas-covered box that makes its appearance, old travellers settling down and making themselves comfortable, fresh ditto and cockneys and every-body abusing everything and vowing they'll go on shore again, etc., etc., etc. As soon as it is possible to get things a little settled, I turn in, and wake up in the morning to find the ship going along at eleven knots with a fair breeze.

We are very grand in the *Benares* as we have a collection of men who call themselves a band on board, and do everything to the sound of a bugle instead of a bell.[9] On Sunday morning we are usually woke up by a chant, generally "Lord Mornington", as being, I suppose, the best morning tune.

By breakfast time, things were getting a little settled, and one is able to see that half a dozen gentlemen and four ladies (properly so called) will about cover the number in the ship, the rest being principally a mixture of cockney vulgarity and colonial impudence very different to the ordinary run of Indian passengers, who are generally men of some stamp. One eats one's breakfast almost in silence, being rather disgusted at the conversation of those around, which is a mixture of grumbling and shop. However, it is best to keep one's ears open as, not being in uniform, people don't mind speaking their mind pretty freely sometimes before one, and it is useful and at the same time amusing to take them down a peg or two quietly now and then.

On this morning after breakfast (the ship going along with a fair wind and all sail set about twelve knots), I sat down to work in the fore saloon, and about half past eleven, just as we were passing through the Straits of Jubal, (the most ticklish navigation of the Red Sea) I was thunderstruck at hearing in the loudest possible speaking trumpet voice, "Ease her." "Stop her." "Turn her astern." Expecting every minute to feel the ship go on shore with a crash, I rushed to my cabin, and put away my papers and went on deck to see what was the matter. The ship was blowing off steam and I could see the people all congregated aft on the starboard side. I then heard the order, "Man overboard, get ready the mail boat." Directly the ship was stopped the boat was let go and pulled away in the direction of the poor fellow who was now about three miles astern, just visible. The sea was running high and the boat could not make much way against it, and long before the boat could get near him he had disappeared altogether, probably pulled under by sharks with which this sea abounds, so there was no help for it but to pick up the lifebuoys and pull on board again. One poor fellow has lost the number of his mess. He is found to be a seedieboy bhandary oxcook. We find that we have lost nearly an hour in stopping to pick him up, and at least fifteen miles of our course, as the ship was going twelve knots, and we turned the ship right round, etc., etc.

It is really quite enough to put one out of all patience to hear how some of these folks do growl, and that without the least reason, some of them evidently trying to find fault. There is a dirty old man on board, a Capt. Milne who had today put on a clean shirt, the second they say since leaving Southampton. He sends a message to the Purser to know if he may have claret at tiffin and tea, as he doesn't drink port, sherry or spirits and the medical men won't let him take hot tea. The Purser gave him permission on these terms. Accordingly at tiffin he has his two tumblers and at dinner three, taking it also in his wineglass to drink with with people, etc.[10]

Now you must know that the P&O pride themselves very much upon their claret, and it is really very good wine. Another passenger was taking claret with him, and said, "This is very nice claret". "Claret, pheugh, it's nothing but vin ordinaire of the very worst description." "Well, I rather like it," the other man said. I overheard this and so addressed the old man at dessert, and said (he had kept a claret bottle in front of him all the time), "May I trouble you for the claret, I think I must have another glass." "H'm, do you like it? I can't think how the P&O can have the face to put such wine on the table." "Indeed," said I, "Do you profess to be a good judge of wine?" "Well, no, I can't say I am, but I'm judge enough to know I don't like that stuff." "Oh, I am surprised to hear that," I said, "for I had noticed that you had taken nothing else." Everybody else had noticed this too, and so there was a general laugh against the old man.

I think he was a good deal put out with me, but has been wonderfully good friends ever since, and I have heard no growling from him. Next day, by the by, he took sherry and madeira as well as claret. You must not put these sort of things down to impudence on my part. I find that it is frequently necessary to take people on a little, but I am never cheeky. I have tried all sorts of ways, and I find that generally if you give in to a man he thinks you are afraid of him and so growls all the more. The Purser is a capital hand at managing refractory people, and I know he has taken one or two down very nicely.

We have not changed Admiralty Agents for the better. The man who went up with us from Bombay, Lt. Slaughter, was a very gentlemanly agreeable man and one who knew his duties, without interfering with other people. The present man (Comr. Keatley) is an old red-faced man, very fond of his grog and particularly great in his own importance, always going to write to the Lords Commissioners of the Admiralty about so and so, etc., etc.

The Purser has sailed with him before and knows how to manage him exactly and I suppose he thought he would try and shew me a little of his importance, as he knew it was no use with him, for he came up to me yesterday morning and pointed to the cabins on the main deck (which are fitted with a W.C. between every two, but which W.C.s are never used as such in a tropical climate). "I desire to know, sir", he said, "why those W.C.s are not in use as such. I see that the stewards use them to keep linen in; that ought not to be allowed." (A question which he had about as much right to ask me as I should have desire to know why he hadn't opened the Mail boxes and taken out all letters addressed to me and other officers of the ship.) I explained to him that those were all very well for vessels running from Southampton, but that in tropical climates we never allowed them to be used except occasionally in the case of great invalids, as the ship would never be clean and sweet, and that there was a W.C. attached to each bathroom besides three others, which were quite enough for all the first-class passengers the ship would carry. "Very well, sir", he replied, after some little more argument, "I shall make a point of writing to the Lords Commissioners of the Admiralty and informing them that on board this ship there are ten water closets not in use." I was so struck with the absurdity of this that I could not help remarking that I was not aware that the Lords Commissioners of the Admiralty took upon themselves the superintendence of the P&O's water closets, whereat he appeared rather riled, and I don't think will bother me about them again. This is perhaps not a very polite incident to quote, but I have done so merely to shew the kind of character one has to deal with, and with all due deference to Admiralty Agents and other extraneous authorities if they interfere where they have no business, they will get their noses burnt.

The *Salsette* with the Bombay mails was to leave Suez two or three hours after us, and her Captain is bent upon beating us to Aden. He is a most fortunate man in passages, as he used to make very quick runs in the *Ottawa*, which nobody else can do at all, and he took the *Manilla* up to China against the monsoon in about two-thirds the time she came down in, with it. I believe his great secret is carrying every stitch of canvas the vessel can spread, and keeping watch on the winds. He borrowed some sails from the *Candia* at Suez, as the *Salsette* has no royals, being only a donkey barque, so then he has the advantage of us; besides he is light and we are rather deep. Yesterday (31st) we just made out his smoke right aft in the early morning and at sunset he was within fifteen or twenty miles of us. The wind fell however during the night, and we have distanced him today as he is hull down on the port quarter. It will be an interesting race, as the two vessels are exact sister ships; in fact the only perceptible difference anywhere is that she has two funnels and we have only one.

April 2nd, Evening

I intended to have finished a long letter on one or two subjects today, but it has been too hot to do anything, and there has been a great deal of excitement all day in the race between the two ships, and I am afraid we must acknowledge ourselves beaten, as she crossed our bows in the most impudent manner this morning about twelve, within biscuit throw, and we have never caught her up yet.

April 11th

I find that on board ship is not at all the place to write many letters for I am always busy all day with the complications of the Purser's accounts, and in the evening one is expected to contribute a share to the general amusement, whatever it be, besides which it is not always the easiest thing to do, when the ship is pitching and rolling about and you don't feel in the humour for thinking much, besides which there is no convenient place, as it is perfectly impossible to write in one's cabin when the ports are shut, and in the saloon there is eating and drinking going on almost perpetually.

Talking of eating and drinking reminds me of a circumstance which I don't think I told you before, and which I was rather amused at, as it gave a (to me) definition of a gentleman. I was talking to an old Indian on the way up, and he said to me, "I knew that you and the Purser were gentlemen before I had ever spoken to either of you, because you both use napkins at dinner". Now a napkin is rather a vanity of mine and I provided myself with some before coming away, and the Purser had done the same, but it shows how people take notice of little things and what trivial matters will tell for and against a man.

I forgot to mention that we were after all ignominiously beaten into Aden by the *Salsette* as she managed somehow or other to dodge us during the night and got in about two hours first, so that we had to wait till she had finished coaling before we began, which was rather a sell and detained us some time.

April 21st

We found that, according to the steward's calculations, we had gained a week by crossing the line as, lo and behold, on the breakfast table appeared a goodly array of hot cross buns as if it were Good Friday. It seems that almost everybody in the ship had been deceived as to its being Good Friday, but most people found out their mistake on the Sunday before. Not so however our good and worthy chief steward, who retained his old opinion of the dates without referring to an almanack and hence the funny results.

It seems that the Australian mail service is to be unfortunate. On arrival we found the *Emeu* with her intermediate shaft broken. It seems that she broke it two days after leaving King George's Sound, and has come for twenty days under sail. However I suppose we shall not have to pay for it, as she was not to be regularly handed over to the P&O Company till her arrival at Suez. The *Granada* took on her mail and passengers, and they would probably reach England by the Calcutta mail, a week after time.

On our arrival a great ugly-looking yellow steamer came up to us with a pilot, and directly we anchored off same, a doctor to examine all the passengers and the crew who had to be mustered accordingly. This is a regular piece of French humbug. Why they should keep up all their French customs in Mauritius is to me a mystery. In addition to about three times the number of passenger lists wanted anywhere else, they require four complete crew lists (which is a bother when there are 218 officers and men on board), also no end of impertinent particulars, such as ages of all the passengers landing, reasons for coming to Mauritius, where born, how long likely to stay in the island, etc., etc., also return of all dogs on board, etc., etc., etc. We had been at anchor about an hour before any communication was allowed, although we brought a clean bill of health from our last port. At last we got through the necessary formalities, and everybody went to shore. We intended to start about nine the next morning and so told people to be on board by that time.

I waited on board for the Purser for about two hours to settle some business before going on shore myself.

After dinner, the Doctor, Chief Officer and myself went on shore and walked around all about the place. There is not much to be seen in the town of Port Louis but it was a great treat to get into such an English place, good straight streets, many of them with good respectable shops on each side, and paved kerb stones, confectioners' shops where one might walk in and buy a tart (unheard of in Bombay), public houses, taverns and hotels too, and all imaginary kinds of shops, the greater number however being a native kind of chandlers in which the principal commodities seemed to be picklebottles, candles and questionable-looking fish, very greasily cooked. I think the greatest treat however was getting a draught of bitter beer from a regular beer engine. I have not tasted anything but bottled beer for so long that this was a great treat. We went into the Roman Catholic Church which is rather a fine building outside but is nothing particular within. It had however a peal of bells that I could stand and listen to for a fortnight.

We returned on board about ten and the next morning I got up about five and went on shore with the Purser and Chief Steward to market. There is a fine large market place but it is very indifferently supplied. We however managed to get a good supply of beef, fresh vegetables and fruit, though at very long prices. The fruits are much the same as Indian ones; bananas, custard apples, pine-apples, water-melons, etc., etc., with the addition of alligator pears, a large fruit something like a pear-shaped mango, and eaten with salt and pepper. Some people liked them pretty well (the Purser glories in them) but I thought them very like walnuts melted in soapsuds with a strong flavour of spermaceti ointment. Certainly the tropical fruits are not to be compared with our own English ones. We got some endive and lettuce and radishes which were a wonderful treat. Although I did not care for salad in England, I can appreciate it now that it is difficult to get. The fish market is like a second Billingsgate and was well supplied with fish, principally mullet and rock cod.

I was rather amused with myself, on meeting a Frenchman who had come out with us, and on his asking me "Parlez-vous français?" I replied "Toro Tora", (Hindustani for 'a little'). I corrected myself directly afterwards, but it was rather ludicrous.

I went on board to breakfast and found the ship would not sail till two, so I went up to the Agents and finished what wanted to be done, and then took another long stroll in a different direction and saw the *Sarah Sands*.[11] On going on board again I found that the men had struck work, having been engaged perpetually for three days and the greater part of three nights coaling the *Emeu, Granada* and ourselves. This being the case, we could not get away till the next morning and so directly after dinner I made one of a party for another exploring expedition, and we took a long walk for some distance outside the town.

Returning about ten o'clock, we were rather hungry after our walk and so thought we would go into the hotel and get some supper. On going inside, however, we found everything shut up and nobody to be seen. With some difficulty, we succeeded in knocking up some of the native waiters and, after waiting half an hour, got some indifferent cold beef and a few other demi-semi-warm leavings of the table d'hôte, with some bread and cheese and beer. For this, one of them had the impudence to give us a bill for $11.75 or about 11/- a head. This was rather too much for what one could get anywhere in England for 1/- or less, so after a good deal of deliberation, we agreed to pay 5/- a head, which we did much to his disgust as I suppose he expected to make a first-rate thing out of us. He certainly was fairly paid, for he must have made at least 3/6d a head out of us. He came on board the next morning to try if he could not get some more, but it was no go.

They are very early people in Port Louis, doing everything by the morning and evening guns which fire about 5 a.m. and 8 p.m. I forgot to mention that I had such a treat on the Saturday morning, going into a regular French hairdressers', and especially after having to put up for a year with those horrid betelnut-chewing, bhang-smelling natives in Bombay who are so thoroughly disgusting that I have frequently endeavoured to cut my own hair rather than submit to them.

We did not get away till the next (Sunday) morning at eleven o'clock. I wish I had known that we should be so long there and I would have ordered my proceedings differently as there are several places, such as Paul and Virginia's Tomb etc., which I should like to have seen, only we arrived there with the idea that twenty-four hours would be the very utmost stay, whereas we were fifty.[12]

We left with every corner of the ship full of coal, and about 240 tons on deck, a not very agreeable thing, but still a necessary nuisance from the length of voyage between Mauritius and King George's Sound. Directly we got well clear of Mauritius we got into strong head winds, the sea running very high and the ship rolling and pitching very uneasily from the great weight on board. For five days our average has been barely six knots, sometimes scarcely five, but on Sunday the wind moderated a little, and we have been picking up. Today (26th) and yesterday it has been much finer and the wind is now veering round abeam, so that we can get fore and aft canvas upon her. It is the first day that we have touched ten knots since the day after leaving, so you can guess what kind of weather we must have had.

It is getting very cold; were it not for the occasional games at quoits, etc., etc., I should be perished, but all the same it is very jolly and I think is doing me good.

68

I had a very narrow escape the other day from losing the sight of an eye. The Doctor had made a small bow and an arrow and was teaching some of the young ideas how to shoot, when he shot an arrow straight into my eye. It stuck there for a second or two before I could make it out, but as soon as I comprehended what the unknown visitor was, I pulled it out and found my eye was not much hurt, as I could see with it though it was a little painful. I bandaged it up to keep the light and cold out and have worn either a bandage or my goggles ever since, leaving them off today for the first time.[13]

May 10th

We made good way with a fair wind till the morning of the third when we sighted land and coasted along near the shore all day. The coast is very like the English Channel from Portland to Plymouth, very bold and in some places covered generally with a kind of scrub. It was rather a treat to see land of any sort after being fifteen days out of sight of it and I think many were not sorry to see a huge bare mass of sandstone, called Cape Baldhead, which marks the entrance to King George's Sound, and to hear "Hard a Starboard", as we passed it and, shortly afterwards, "Ease her, Stop her", and up went blue lights and rockets for a pilot. I should think the old screw began to scratch its head and think what could possibly be the matter for he had been hard at it for so long, that it must have seemed rather strange to have found himself so quiet again.

The pilot would not take us up alongside the hulk that night as there were a good many ships in the place and the navigation was intricate, so we dropped anchor for the night and, in the morning, at daylight went on into the harbour.

Directly after breakfast, the first thing to be done was to go on shore, and everybody went. It was such a treat to be pulled about by English boatmen and the charge was not out of the way, only 1/-.

Directly one got on shore, the first things to be seen were two or three savages, daubed all over with red ochre, who saluted us with "Good Morning, Sir", which is, I believe, considered equivalent to 6d, then saying, "Shall I show you the place, sir?", supposed to be equivalent to 1/-. Had we accepted their proffered services, a pound would have been thought far too little for it. As at most other places which I have been to, at King George's Sound the natives evidently labour under the popular delusion that Englishmen are made of money for, from the Somalies at Aden who swim about in the water and sing out "Hiv somefin master", "Sikkurspence pliz master", etc., to the men holding high appointments in India, one always finds that

69

they expect the sahibs to be rolling in wealth or, at any rate, profess to do so.

We found our way to the only Hotel in the place kept by a very respectable-looking Englishman, and looking like a small country roadside inn at home, when we were beset by a crowd of these savages, the most horrid-looking wretches I have ever seen, daubed all over their bodies with red ochre and white paint, demi-semi-dressed in sheepskins and opossum skins, and carrying their spears and boomerangs about with them. I saw some of them do most wonderful things with their spears: they would hit a sixpence at from thirty to forty yards distant, and would throw their boomerangs for an immense distance. One of our passengers very narrowly escaped having his head taken off by a return boomerang. They are certainly most formidable weapons as they come with an immense force and are as sharp as any sword. After some time, these fellows got up a "caraberie" or war dance which we went into the bush to see. It was a most curious performance and the noises they made were something awful sometimes.

Mr Brown holds an opinion (rather an unfortunate one) that he can play upon the French Horn and, as his cabin was next to mine, I used frequently to disabuse him of his opinion on the subject. One morning, as the Purser and I were hard into some abstruse calculations, he began an unearthly tune when I ejaculated, "There's our horny friend again," whereat the Purser, who has a strong sense of the ridiculous, kept on laughing the whole morning, and he has gone by the name of "our horny friend" ever since.

We got off the Heads at about eleven and lay to discharging the Tasmanian mails into another steamer till nearly twelve, when we started up Hobsons Bay. Going up we passed the Black Ball Clipper *Lightning*, the fastest sailing ship afloat, that made the passage home round the Horn in sixty three days. It was a beautiful sight to see her with all her canvas spread, going down the Bay at about ten knots an hour. Another Black Ball Clipper, *Rowena*, was outside as we went up.

We got alongside the coal ship in Melbourne Harbour at about a quarter past three and then came all the bidding goodbye.

May 12th
We got away from the hulk at about one this morning. We are now going about thirteen knots, fair wind and all sail set. The ship seems quite desolate now, only one lady on board and two or three gentlemen.

70

May 14th, at Sydney

8am. Arrived at Sydney Heads after a very quick passage of 48 and a half hours from Port Phillip Heads. Took in pilot and steamed on through the Heads.

One can well imagine Captain Cook disbelieving in the existence of anything more than a "boat harbour" inside, as, until quite close in, nothing more is visible than a narrow opening between two huge perpendicular cliffs of 300 feet in height, which do not look very inviting to approach too closely, as there is a heavy surf continually beating against them, and should a ship approach too near, there is but small chance for her, as was proved in the case of the unfortunate *Dunbar*.[14]

On getting between the Heads, however, the most beautiful prospect imaginable is opened out, a large harbour with innumerable bays on either side. There are but few ships visible from the mouth of the harbour, as they are nearly all positioned a long way up round the corner, and in other positions where they are not visible from the Heads. In fact, I believe it would be an easy matter to anchor every ship belonging to Europe in Sydney Harbour, so that none of them should be visible from a ship between the Heads. The beauty of the prospect in steaming up the harbour is very great. At every turn some fresh bay opens out, disclosing new beauties and making one think "What a Paradise this is!"

Steamed on up the Harbour past H.M. ships *Iris* and *Cordelia* past Government House, a fine large building very prettily situated, overlooking Woolloomooloo Bay and the men-of-war, past Circular Quay with its numbers of large ships, up to Moore's wharf where we dropped anchor, close to the *Columbian* which was waiting to take the mails on to Suez; dipped ensigns, of course, in passing. Landed our mails at nine thirty and bid adieu to the remaining passengers.

At two p.m. the *Columbian* fired her gun, dipped her ensign and was off. At six the *Wonga Wonga*, a clipper colonial steamer, arrived from Melbourne having left with the notion that she would have been in before the *Benares* (as these steamers knowing everything of the coast can keep close inland and so gain a great deal of distance and avoid the currents and, being fast steamers, generally beat the mail very considerably). She had gained only about two hours on us, at which her Captain was rather wild, having, I believe, laid a good deal of money on it.

Went on shore after dinner with Doctor and Chief Engineer. Very much surprised to find such a large and well-built place, second to few, if any, in England, except London. The principal street, George Street, is, they say,

71

three miles long and has some very fine shops in it. It is a wide, well-arranged street, more like New Oxford Street than any other in London, or High Street, Southampton. Then there are Pitt and Castlereagh Streets, both large, handsome streets with good shops and many fine buildings. The Banks and other buildings are some of them very handsome and the Exchange will bear comparison with any building in England, out of London. There are several other very fine streets crossing the others at right angles (a great improvement on the irregular style of many of the London streets) and many smaller streets, squares, places, terraces and so forth.

Being Saturday night, there was a good deal of bustle in the streets and the market was rather an interesting sight. Most of the articles were very cheap, meat selling at 1d a pound (such meat as would be worth 2/- or 3/- a pound in Bombay), plenty of vegetables and a good deal of fruit though the fruit season was nearly over. We bought some peaches at 1/- a dozen, which could hardly be considered out of the way, and then went to the Theatre. There are two theatres in the place and the one we went to was a very pretty little one, well fitted up. The acting was very good and the audience respectable, though there was but small amount of beauty among the ladies.

May 15th

In the morning went to Church with the Chief Officer at St. James, an old red brick building, very badly arranged inside, the pews high and narrow, no bookstand or hassocks and no communion table. The service, however, tolerably well conducted. It was a great treat to get into a church once again after having been three months without entering one.

After service, we took a walk round the Domain and Botanical Gardens. We noticed a great many plants too numerous to describe and, after a very pleasant walk (a great treat for me in the middle of the day), got back to the ship in time for dinner. After dinner, went to St. Phillip's Church (a rather prettily-arranged church with a square tower, a little like St. John's at Lewisham) with Chief Engineer.

May 16th

Took a very pretty walk in the afternoon and went to the Theatre in the evening to see Macbeth.

May 17th

Took a walk through the town and Botanical Gardens with Doctor.

72

May 18th

At Accounts all day and did not leave the ship.

May 19th

Went for a sail down the harbour with Doctor and Fourth Officer in the lifeboat.

May 20th

Took dinghy and went fishing and pulling with the Doctor. No very great luck as the Doctor would not stick to fishing.

Evening, went up to Waterview Bay on board the *Australasian* with Purser and Doctor, taking an oar myself. Had not had so much pulling for many a long day.

May 21st

Blowing very hard all day. Evening went on shore with Purser and Doctor to see Anderson, the Wizard of the N. Was much amused at his tricks which are, many of them, extremely clever. He has a little daughter, about fourteen years old, who has a wonderful memory and a clever knack of spelling any words backwards as well as forwards.

May 22nd

Morning and Evening church at St. Phillip's with Captain. A long walk between morning service and dinner.

May 23rd

In the evening, received the intelligence of the *Columbian* having broken down and put back to Adelaide for repairs. What a pity! The second purchase of the Company for the Australian Line broken down in the same manner as the first; the mails almost certain to be a long while after date in arrival at London.

May 24th

Queen's Birthday. A grand day in Sydney, no end of regattas, picnics, excursions, etc., on foot, the principal attraction being Manly Beach, where there was a grand regatta going on, steamers crowded with holiday folks continually passing to and fro.

Went out exploring creeks, etc., with Doctor and Chief Engineer in dinghy.

At 7 p.m. just going down to tea and heard a crash somewhere, followed by an attempt at a scream. Rushed up on deck and found that two steamers had managed to come into collision just under our bows. The Chief Officer sang out "D'ye want any assistance". "No thank ye," was the answer. However, boats were lowered and pulled up to see if they could be of any use. I was much amused at the *sang froid* with which they seemed to treat the matter, just as if it were an ordinary occurrence. There was no abuse, no "Why didn't you do so and so?", but just "Oh, you've cut my paddle wheel in two, just haul alongside and give us a tow". "Aye, aye".

At ten minutes to eight had a candle lit in each port and the venetian drawn in front of it, a man sent out to each yard armed with a supply of blue lights and another to the end of each boom. At the first stroke of eight bells up went a rocket from each side, and the venetians were drawn on one side and the blue lights struck simultaneously. The effect was the prettiest illumination that had ever been seen in Sydney. Crowds were running down from all parts to look at the ship, and everyone pronounced it perfect. The *Benares* has very large ports very near the water and the lights make her look an immense length. The blue lights at the yard arm had, as they always have, a very pretty effect. At the first stroke of ten every light in the ship was doused at once, the signal being four rockets. I may here mention that our rockets, which are some of the best I ever saw, were the only respectable ones in the place; there were several attempts at fireworks, etc., but all very meagre after ours.

May 25th

Spent the day catching mackerel.

May 26th

Tug came alongside, up anchor and were towed up to Cockatoo Island to be docked in the Government dock there.[15] Got all settled in dock and the caisson in by 3 p.m.

Found we were in a place apparently completely landlocked but with a very pretty prospect on every side. Cockatoo Island itself has not much beauty about it but it is admirably adapted for the purpose to which it is applied, viz., a receptacle for convicts and a Government Dock. The dock is a very fine one and when it is extended (as the purpose doing to the length of upwards of 400 feet) it will be one of the finest docks in existence. It is principally excavated out of the solid rock and is all convict labour. Sydney is a capital place for building for you can generally build a house with the stone which you cut out from the foundation. It reminds me very much of old times to be in dock with convicts working all round.[16]

May 28th

There is a fine Hotel standing in the middle of gardens very nicely laid out and containing specimens of all the birds and beasts peculiar to Australia, besides a few lions, tigers, etc., and other animals peculiar to India, America, etc.

Some of the birds are very pretty and curious: there was a large black cockatoo, several black swans (and there used to be a white crow, but he is dead), several very beautiful specimens of Australian parrots of various sorts and colours. The most curious bird that I have ever seen is I think the "Laughing Jackass", a kind of parrot which makes the most absurd noises you can conceive, hooting and screaming and jabbering and then going off into peals of laughter, so that it is almost impossible to keep one's countenance. There are a great many in the neighbourhood of Sydney and I should like to have brought one away, only it would make such a noise that I could not well keep it on board ship. Then there were the pretty kangaroos, which do look a little out of proportion with their immensely long hind legs and their short fore legs, but looking very pretty leaping and jumping along. Then emus, large birds something like an ostrich with a turkey's head. Their heads are between five and six feet from the ground and they have immense power, can run very fast and their kick is as bad as a horse's. The dingoes, or native dogs, are very fine animals and when tamed I believe very faithful. They have a head like a wolf and are altogether something like the Esquimaux dogs.

We walked a little way along the sea shore and saw from a little distance La Perouse's monument and, after seeing everything else there was to be seen, we returned to the Barracks. Colonel Percival kindly asked me to stay to dinner but I thought I had better not as the baby was poorly and so I walked down the town, getting a chop at a restaurant on my way.

I was very much pleased with my trip to Botany Bay, but I wonder they don't change its name as it is always associated in the minds of Englishmen with convicts (I beg their pardon, Government men) although not a single convict was ever landed there, nor has it ever been a convict place.

Many of the most wealthy men in Sydney have either themselves left their country for their country's good or their fathers have done so before them, and I find that it is not considered at all good taste in Sydney society to go back as far as a man's grandfather (particularly among old inhabitants), in conversation. There are none of the original convicts at Cockatoo Island, they are now all men who have been convicted for colonial offences. Sydney people never speak of "convicts"; they are always either "Government men", "men who were sent out", "men who had a free passage given to them" or something of that description.

May 29th

Went over to Sydney with Doctor and went to Christ Church, a very nice church indeed with a large congregation. Very nicely-conducted services and a good preacher.

May 30th

After breakfast went with the Captain, Chief Officer, Purser and Doctor by steamer up to Parramatta, a place about twenty miles away from Sydney.

The scenery along the sides of the harbour on the way up is most beautiful, in many places quite like Swiss scenery, beautiful bays opening up at every turn, some of them very wild-looking and others beautifully laid out and nicely cultivated along their sides with groves of orange trees, etc., here and there. There are some very nice houses along the water's edge, some of them in the most lovely situations, tempting me very strongly to wish to be a colonial millionaire. The town of Parramatta is very like some old country village in England. There are several old-fashioned-looking large brick houses, a few general shops, three places of worship, an English Church, Romish and Wesleyan or Scotch (I am not sure which), a large orphan asylum, and the inevitable adjunct to all Australian towns, a jail or, as it is usually denominated, an "Institution". We had tiffin at a regular old-fashioned country inn, with some of the nicest fresh butter I have tasted for many a long day, and returned to Cockatoo Island in time for a late dinner.

On arrival at Cockatoo Island we found that during our absence a convict, nick-named "Jack in the Box" from his having once made his escape on board a ship inside a large box, had got away, and the general idea was that he had probably concealed himself on board the ship, disguised as a Lascar, particularly as he had left his old clothes behind him where he had been working. The ship consequently put under strict surveillance and nobody allowed to leave her without a countersign. At midnight he was pricked up with a bayonet, lying under the lee of a large rock, all ready for a swim over to the opposite shore, having dressed himself entirely in white, so that he could hardly be distinguished from one of the great masses of rock which lie all along the beach.

76

May 31st

Working all day, dinner party on board in the evening, consisting of the officials at Cockatoo Island, the Captain of the *Oneida* and a few friends of the Captain's. Tasted kangaroo soup for the first time, capital stuff it is too. Had a bit of a dance in the evening after dinner.

June 1st

After tiffin, took the dinghy and went with Chief Engineer and Fourth Officer to Spectacle Island oystering. Ate enough oysters for half a dozen fellows on ordinary occasions; such beautiful plump little fellows, it makes my mouth water to think of them for I had not tasted a raw oyster since I left England.

June 2nd

Ascension Day. Morning, went with Captain Scottowe and Mr. Moore, the Agent, to St. Andrew's temporary Cathedral. Heard an excellent sermon from the Bishop of Sydney, a man who stands about six feet five and is, therefore, facetiously called a High Churchman, though his doctrines are, I should imagine, very different to those of Dr. Pusey. Afternoon took an omnibus out to Redfern.

June 3rd

Directly after breakfast started with Chief Officer for a walk to the South Head. Was not in good trim for a long walk having slightly galled my heel the day before from walking in a new pair of boots. However, it was a long-promised affair and I would not give in, so with a packet of sandwiches in each pocket, a "pocket pistol" in my breast pocket and my drinking cup over my shoulder, off I started, having first taken the precaution of soaping my socks inside after the most approved system. Parish provided himself similarly, only with a telescope instead of a drinking cup slung across his shoulder.

Away we trudged through Woolloomooloo, skirting all the Bays on the south side of the Harbour, and now and then getting the most lovely peeps I have ever seen. We walked up to the Lighthouse and went up to the top of it. The cliffs on which this Lighthouse stands are like a perpendicular wall, upwards of 300 feet above the sea, which dashes against their feet with a loud roar. It was rather giddy work looking down from the edge at the sea underneath.

We stood over the place where the *Dunbar* was wrecked and had the

77

whole circumstances explained to us by the man in charge of the Light-house, a very intelligent man, who gave us also a good deal of information about the working of the lights, etc. It seems that the only living being that knew anything about the wreck till the next morning was a fine large Newfoundland dog who has lived at the Lighthouse for years, and which ran out and stood barking at the top of the cliff for some time. There was, as you are doubtless aware, only one man saved, and how he escaped is a mystery; a most miraculous escape without doubt.

We walked back the same way as we came and got on board about six, after a walk of about twenty miles. I found my heel rather sore on getting back and next morning could not get a boot on that foot. Unable to leave the ship for four days in consequence of heel not being healed (no pun intended).

June 7th
Northam arrived at Melbourne with mails, after a capital passage down, and left for Sydney at 2 p.m. Showed my foot to Doctor, who pronounced that I had a large abscess on my heel, which he accordingly dug into and gave me instant relief.

June 8th
Evening went with Doctor and Purser to the Theatre and saw John Drew, the Irish comedian. A most amusing fellow who kept us in peals of laughter the whole evening.

June 9th
Still lame but better.

June 10th
Northam was signalled, so went on board at twelve as she came in to ask for letters.

Called on Mr. Stephen, a barrister, and promised to go up to his office the next morning to go over the University with him or his brother. Called on Sir Alfred Stephens, the Chief Justice, who was not at home, and Mr. Dias Thomson, the Colonial Secretary, who seemed to be extremely agreeable.

June 11th
Went on board *Oneida* and to Royal Mail Office to see about passage to Melbourne. Was informed that the ship would sail punctually at 4 o'clock.

Went up to Mr. Stephen's office and he sent me over to his father's to see his brother, who would go over the University with me. Went to Sir Alfred Stephens' and found him at home. He gave me a most warm welcome and said he would go with me as well. He first of all took me to the Museum, a very nice one though not very large. I was much interested in some of the curiosities there, particularly the ancient weapons, etc., of the natives of Australia and New Zealand, and the stuffed animals and birds peculiar to the country, most of which I had never seen before. We then went over to the College in connection with the University and of which Sir Alfred is one of the Trustees. It is a very pretty building with comfortable rooms for the students, a handsome hall, a very pretty little chapel, and very comfortable arrangements altogether.

After going over the College, we went to the University which is as yet only about half finished, but when completed will be a magnificent building. The hall is a splendid room with several beautiful stained-glass windows, three of which are very fine ones. The carved work, both in wood and stone, is all most beautifully done and I don't think I ever saw a building so elaborately finished. Went over the library, a fine room with a very good collection of books, and was introduced to the Librarian.

I was obliged rather to hurry away as I had determined to go down to Melbourne in the *Oneida,* and she was to sail at four o'clock. You can imagine my disgust, on getting down to the Royal Mail Office, to see a notice stuck up that the *Oneida* would not leave till noon the next day. However, there was no help for it, so I went on board to dinner, and spent the evening on board the *Northam.*

June 12th, on board *Oneida*

Went on board *Oneida* at ten a.m. At noon ship cast off, and finally started about half past one. Pilot left off the Heads about three, and away we steamed.

The *Oneida* is a splendid large steamer, but I don't like her arrangements as well as that of P&O steamers. She has a large poop and is lumbered up everywhere with deckhouses, etc., besides which she has no ports to her cabins, only scuttles, and then again they have that pothouse system with regard to wines, which I abominate. You call for a pint of beer or a bottle of sherry and have to write down on a card what you want. Then after you have had enough you stick your card into the cork and it is put up into a swinging rack above the table till next meal. If you ask a person to take wine you have to send your bottle, etc., and they make you pay through the nose for everything. Altogether I dislike the system immensely and I think the P&O plan is far better and in the end cheaper.

The Purser of the *Oneida* is a very fine fellow, whom I had met in Bombay and, knowing the Captain, I fared very well.

June 15th, at Melbourne

Arrived off Port Phillip Heads one a.m. and anchored till daylight. Dropped anchor in Hobson's Bay at 11.20 a.m. and went on shore in small steamer. Took a car up to Melbourne and went to P&O office, left my bag and some letters, and had some tiffin with Denham.

Found my way to Uncle Henry's office, was told he had gone to the Crown Lands Office, went to the Crown Lands Office and was referred to the Penal Settlements Office. Went to the Penal Settlements Office and was referred back to his own office. Went again to his own office, found he had not returned but probably would during the day. Went again to the Crown Lands Office but with no better success. Returned to his own office and, finding he was not there, waited until four o'clock when I went back to the P&O Office, got my bag and took a car out to South Yarra. Found his house without difficulty as he had given me ample directions. He had come home and was expecting me and both Aunt Maria and he gave me a most cordial welcome.

I was much pleased with Uncle Henry's house which is, I think, about the most sensible one I have seen in the colony. It has not many rooms but they are all a nice size and, what is of most importance, a good height; I should think they were thirteen and a half or fourteen feet high. A large dining room and drawing room with two large bedrooms and a dressing room, all on one floor. Underneath, kitchens, scullery, servant's bedroom, laundry, etc., and a very good second spare room for a makeshift, plenty of good cupboards and every convenience with a regular Indian verandah all round three sides of the house.

I tasted some Colonial Hock at Dinner, really a most delicious light wine, a great deal better than very much which is sold as "Hock" in England.

June 16th

Took a walk round the garden the first thing with Uncle Henry. They have a very nice flower garden with all our English flowers growing most luxuriantly, the borders principally geraniums and violets, both of which grow in great profusion. Breakfasted off a cold Tasmanian fowl the size of a Bombay turkey and most delicious eating.

After breakfast went out with Aunt Maria for a walk and called on General MacArthur, the Commander-in-Chief. There are some very pretty views all round and I was surprised at the extent of the place. Returned to tiffin and afterwards went with Aunt Maria to the Botanical Gardens, which are very pretty though not so well laid out yet as the Sydney ones.

I went into Melbourne by boat down the Yarra Yarra and went with Uncle Henry over the Public Library, Houses of Parliament, etc. The former is a most wonderful place, containing already some 13,000 volumes which will be increased to 25,000, and any person is at liberty to go in and read any book he likes, simply putting his name down as he goes in. They say that there are already more people who go there every day than to the Library of the British Museum. It is without doubt a great thing to have an institution of the sort in a place like Melbourne and I only wish they had one in Bombay. The Houses of Parliament are inside very handsome but I did not admire the outside much. They are hardly finished yet but the building looks heavy and dull, built of that eternal ironstone, of which there is a great deal in Melbourne, capital stuff for roads but does not, for my taste at least, look well in a large building unless relieved by some lighter material. Returned to South Yarra by train.

A small dinner party consisting of Mr. & Mrs. Murray Smith and Mr. Tyler of the Customs, all very great friends, and a Captain and Mrs. Hall. We had a pleasant evening with music, etc., and I could quite imagine myself in England again. It was such a treat to me to get alongside a fire again that the first night I was in Melbourne, I could scarcely do anything else but poke it all the evening and put coals on, etc.

June 17th, on board *Benares*

Said goodbye to Aunt Maria about ten past eleven with a great many regrets that I could not stay a month instead of two days with them.

Went with Uncle Henry for a walk through all the principal streets, etc. Found the *Benares* was in the Bay and would sail again during the night, so made arrangements to go on board about five. Uncle Henry had to return to his office for a short time so I was left to my own devices. Executed a few shopping commissions, etc., and met an old schoolfellow, who was expelled from the school for housebreaking about two years before I left.

Went off to the *Benares* a little past five after saying goodbye to Uncle Henry. Was introduced by Uncle Henry to a young squatter named Gladstone, who is going to England, cousin of the Mr. Gladstone and a very nice fellow.

June 18th

We got under way about daylight and dropped the Pilot off the Heads about 10.30 a.m.

I should very much like to have seen more of Melbourne but of course it couldn't be managed. It is an immense place and the streets are very wide, wider than almost any in London. It is a frightfully 'go-ahead' place; nobody would conceive it possible that within the last six years it could be possible for such a place to spring up as it has done, and it is still progressing rapidly. It very much corresponds with my idea of a Yankee city; there is a great deal of that independent kind of vulgarity and 'sharp business practice' that one scarcely sees except among the Americans and, though there are of course many nice people and good honest men, yet it seems to me that the 'snobocracy' decidedly predominate.

Denham complains that the merchants and others with whom he has to deal are all Jews and Scotchmen, so that he has to look pretty sharp about him. There are few, if any, nice people anywhere than the set in which Uncle Henry moves, but I should imagine they are the exception rather than the rule in Melbourne society. This will, I daresay, improve in time as people with good fixed appointments and high positions go out there.

They have generally one or two English men-of-war of their own, a little screw corvette called the *Victoria*. As, however, the English Government don't allow privateering, whenever the vessel is sent anywhere where it is thought likely that there will be fighting, the officers have all to be sworn in as Special Constables. Their uniform is exactly the same as the English Navy, only silver instead of gold, so that when in full dress they look more like policemen than Naval officers. Talking of police, they have a very fine body of them at Melbourne, both mounted and on foot. They were originally embodied for the protection of gold escorts from the diggings, and have proved themselves useful on more occasions than one.

Arrived off the entrance of the Straits between Kangaroo Island and the mainland on Sunday at 8 p.m. after a very quick passage indeed.

The alteration which was made in the pitch of the screw at Sydney has certainly made a marked improvement in the ship's speed, we steam faster with fewer revolutions.

Waited till the moon got up and then steamed into Nepean Bay, taking them by surprise. Very rough weather but the wind pretty fair.

June 22nd

3 a.m. Ship rolling considerably; the coals in the starboard bunkers discovered to be on fire, very fortunately discovered in time, and put out before any of the passengers were awake. It was most providential that it was discovered so soon as, had it gained on the ship, nobody knows what might have become of us all. Fire is at all times a dreadful thing, particularly with the other elements to contend with as well. Thanks to the good discipline of the ship and the many appliances at hand and ready, the fire was got under without anyone on board, except those immediately concerned, knowing anything of it. The first I knew of it was noticing that the deck had been broken up in several places, as I went aft to the saloon to breakfast.

June 24th

7 a.m. Arrived at King George Sound after a very good passage. Went on shore for a walk, gathered some wild flowers as a last remembrance of Australia and got on board to dinner.

Left the Sound about 8 p.m. and for the next three days encountered a heavy gale of wind with a very high sea, the ship labouring very much. When lying in bed (my berth is athwartships) I was sometimes standing on my head and then suddenly on my feet, very rarely being in anything like a horizontal position, my cabin a confused mass of boxes, clothes, books, toothbrushes, boots, flowers, papers, bedding, hats, brushes, etc., etc., etc., ad inf.

The dinner table was an amusing scene (with small attendance however), the consumption of crockery and victuals being in an inverse ratio to the usual average, a regular case of "eat what you can, while you can get it, and don't be particular".

A man was just going to attempt to carve a heart, when it took a dive off the dish and lodged at the door of a cabin of children, whereupon he was of course accused of losing his heart to one of the young ladies inside, etc., etc. Very uncomfortable weather because impossible to do anything. Walking, reading, writing, thinking, eating, drinking and, with many people, even sleeping, quite out of the question.

June 28th

Light breeze, still with heavy swell.

June 29th

Beautiful weather with light fair wind (almost too light to be good). Every available stitch of canvas set and everything comfortable.

July 8th

At Port Louis 1.30 p.m. Got news of war in Europe. Evening went to Opera and saw Lucia de Lammermoor.

July 9th

Went to market early and on board to breakfast, had hair cut, etc. 2.30 p.m. left Mauritius. Fair weather with strong breezes up to Aden.

July 12th

I have been altogether very much pleased indeed with my visit to Australia. It is indeed a wonderful country and I don't wonder at people settling there and never wishing to go home again. I should think either Melbourne or Sydney a good place for a young man with a tolerably good, certain appointment, provided he could get good introductions, but not otherwise. I myself would be glad to go there tomorrow, were the P&O to give me the offer of an appointment there, for the good colonial people are a very nice agreeable society, though I cannot say I like the generality much.[17]

I cannot say I like a Purser's life on board ship much. I never did, or I would have chosen it long ago, but I don't think I am likely to be called upon to serve in that way, except in a case of great emergency and it is always as well to know as much as possible. We have hitherto had an extremely pleasant voyage up, the speed of the ship is much increased by the pitch of the screw being altered, and we have been most fortunate in the weather with the exception of the gales we encountered off the Leewin.

The passengers are altogether a very agreeable set of people, and though there are a few who dispense almost entirely with forks at dinner and who drop their h's and murder Her Majesty's English, yet there some very gentlemanly and clever men on board. We have dropped the greater number of them at Mauritius and all the ladies have gone, but we were a very pleasant party coming up.

I see they have got the Telegraph laid down the Red Sea as far as Aden. This is a grand thing and I suppose it will not be long now before it is opened the whole way to Bombay. You will probably see our arrival at Aden telegraphed long before you get this. I wish I could go as a telegram and join the ship again in Aden.

The general news from Europe is as I had feared and expected. War to the knife between France and Austria.[18] I only hope and trust that England may be able to steer clear of it. In case of a war with France, one of the first places threatened would be The Mauritius. There is always a large French fleet at Bourbon, and we have one solitary gunboat and a few guns mounted indifferently at Port Louis, besides which I think the native population are far better disposed towards the French than ourselves.

I see by the papers that Parliament has been dissolved and that the Squire is in again for Cornwall without opposition. I notice that Waguelin is out for Southampton.[19]

After all that I have heard of Alfred, I was scarcely surprised at the intelligence conveyed in his letter to you. His remarrying so soon was hardly a matter of surprise to me after all I have heard of his doings since his arrival in England. For my own part, I should think that in common decency and in respect to his late wife and her relations he ought to have waited at least another year.

July 18th

We arrived at Aden yesterday early in the morning and got away at night. We found the *Malta* lying there disabled, in consequence of which the *Benares* will, I expect, have to go down from Suez to Australia, lying at Suez a month without going to Bombay at all.

There is an old proverb that "misfortunes never come singly", and this seems to be thoroughly exemplified in our steamers. First the *Emeu* breaks down, then the *Columbian* and *Malta*, the *Nemesis* runs over a steamer and kills forty people, the *Bengal* gets on shore on the coast of Ceylon, necessitating the *Ganges* being sent up to Calcutta instead of her, the *Malabar* breaks down in the China Seas, and is reported everywhere as foundered at sea, and last but not by any means least, the *Alma*, one of our crack ships, is totally wrecked in the Red Sea. This last will be a very heavy blow to the Company.

I fell across Hugh Miller's Testimony of the Rocks at Col. Percival's and mean to get it with several other books when I once get settled again.[20] I have been reading a little Mercantile Law since I left Bombay, but I find that a ship is not the place either to read or write much except in the calmest of weather.

It has been fearfully hot since leaving Aden, hotter than ever I felt in Bombay I think and impossible to sleep at night except on deck.

July 29th, At Suez

The last two or three days have been nothing but bilgewater, work and noise, but in a day or two I hope to take a trip over to Cairo when my work is finished. It seems tantalising to be within nine days of dear old England, particularly now that dear old Ted is home, and yet not able to get any nearer.

I am afraid things look rather warlike but I do hope we shall be able to keep out of it.

August 9th

Here I am still within the tantalising distance of a nine days' run from England and not yet able to get any nearer.

Suez is a peculiarly lively place. We lie so far from the shore that it is a three hour business each way from shore to ship, and when on shore there is nothing to be done unless to eat a slice of water-melon and smoke a 'shee-shee' or 'hubble-bubble' with a friend. There is plenty of work of one sort or another to be done on board. As a natural consequence, one can rarely or never leave the ship and when on board one dares not look much over the side for fear of being totally blinded with the glare.

Then the water which one gets from the shore is brackish and the distilled water made on board is very like train oil. There is one consolation, however, that things might be a great deal worse at Aden. For instance, the heat just now would be altogether unbearable, while here it is deliciously cool directly the sun goes down, although the thermometer during the day approaches very near to three figures in the shade. In the Red Sea the temperature of the water was generally ninety-one, a tolerably warm bath in England, and here during the daytime it is I think as hot or nearly so.

The *Cyclops* is lying within a cable's length of us and I see Captain Pullen sometimes. I dined with him yesterday.

We have just experienced the delights of a regular simoon which does not tend to improve the temper. Sand in face, in hands, in hair, sand all over everywhere. Although a considerable distance off the land, the wind as hot as it is possible to conceive, something like walking head to wind along a very dusty road in England after the particles of dust had been ground up to one thousandth part of their usual size, and passed through a hot oven, and the wind coming from the very back of the same furnace. It came on suddenly as possible just after dinner and now that it is over it is so hot and sultry that breathing, to say the least of it, is difficult.

We passed a wrecked steamer coming up the sea (The *"IforgetwhatyoucallherbutaregularcrackjawEgyptianname"*) which we thought at first was the *Emeu*. She was deserted by her crew directly she struck without any attempt to get her off. The men all walked up across the Desert to Suez, a long distance. The last man, the engineer, an Englishman, arrived the other day, having been left for dead and picked up by some Coptic priests going down to fish. They took him to their convent and next morning there was a cool request sent in from the sheik for his head, as being a trespasser. However, the priests took care of him, and sent him away with his head on his shoulders and he is now recovering fast from the effects of the hardships which he underwent.

What would I give for a sherry cobbler or an ice pudding just now! There is no such luxury as ice in Suez.

August 17th, at Cairo

A little nearer still to England. I came across yesterday afternoon with Captain Scottowe and the Doctor and Purser to spend a day or two here.

It seems so curious to be travelling in a railway train over probably the same track of the Israelites for some distance, and one cannot help thinking what would they have thought could they have seen a huge train approaching them at the rate of twenty or twenty-five miles an hour. It is an immense improvement having the railway open all the way through and one can now come across from Suez to Cairo with as much ease as from Southampton to London.

We arrived last evening in time for a wash and some dinner and shall probably stay until Saturday. I want, if possible, to go to the pyramids, but as they have just opened the floodgates of the Nile for the annual irrigation, I fear it will be a work of some difficulty.

This morning we got up early and mounted our Arab steeds to ride through the Bazaar and up to the Citadel. We saw the Grand Hall there, a superb room, a mixture of grandeur and sham, being partly built of most beautiful marble and partly painted to represent it. We saw the place where the Mameluke took his desperate leap and it is positively miraculous that he was not dashed to pieces.[21] Fancy a man jumping down on horse-back from the top of the cross of St. Paul's Cathedral (this is, I believe, higher) and escaping unhurt. His horse was, of course, killed under him.

I think you would laugh to see me riding donkey-back along the narrow lanes here, frequently in danger of being crushed between some camel with a load of stones and a bullock-cart or other hard substance, sitting as far aft as possible, and profiting from my experience in Alexandria last year, eschewing stirrups altogether. I always adopt the humane principle embodied in the first two lines of the well-known verse "If I had a donkey, etc", and finds it answers much better, generally speaking. I do hate to have a lot of small boys after me thumping away on the poor donkey and making him slew round in all imaginable ways, and generally administer a clout on the head of anyone who will persist in banging the poor donkey. I apply a little wholesome correction with my heels to his sides now and then and, if I have anything like a decent animal, find that I generally keep at the head of all banged bucks. It is wonderful the fatigue which these little animals will undergo. On the way out, you may remember they all went twenty-five miles through the hot sand in the middle of the day with a big soldier on the back of each, and they would go back the same day and be as fresh as possible the next morning.

Cairo is very much like all Oriental towns, but has some very pretty scenery all round. There are also some very fine large buildings and pretty gardens, avenues, etc., which one has to whistle for in Bombay.

It is just now the hottest season of the year and tolerably warm it is (from 89 to 97 in the shade); we had it 106 the other day in Suez, but it is a very dry heat and a more healthy kind of heat than the Indian. The heat from the reflected sand in the desert is very great, and if you attempt to walk half a dozen steps your feet are scorched. The glare too, is of course very great, and nearly all the natives here suffer more or less with opthalmia.

August 23rd

I dined with our Agent, Frank Whitely, a very nice fellow (brother to the one in Bombay and a great improvement on him) and drove out with him to Schubra Gardens, a beautifully laid out place about five miles from Cairo. There is a magnificent kiosk or summer house in these gardens of immense size.

In the afternoon, the passengers ex *Indus* arrived and among them I found an old schoolfellow and chum named Wilton, who has left Oxford for the sake of a commission in the Army. I took a walk with him through some of the bazaar and was much amused at the astonishment which he manifested at the oriental dirt and bad odours in lieu of the luxurious kind of fairy London which he seemed to expect. They left the next morning at daylight and I rode out to the Petrified Forest, a wonderful collection of petrified logs of wood, evidently the remains of a large forest.

In the evening, I was introduced to Hakikhan Bey, an Armenian I think, a very clever man but one with a few very strange theories. Among others, he has a plan of coating the Electric Cable with gold and glass, etc., etc., etc.[22]

We returned to Suez the following morning, well pleased with our trip, and on Monday morning early, the *Madras* came in from Bombay bringing me orders from Mr Ritchie to proceed to Singapore as Assistant to Gardner Jellicoe, who is Agent there. This is the appointment of all others in the service which I fancy I shall most like.

I have determined on proceeding down as far as Aden in the *Benares*, thence on the *Madras* to Bombay, and after staying three or four days, then proceed at once to Singapore.

Latest news. Midnight. *Northam* a total wreck off Djeddah. We are just off at once to render assistance. No lives lost. Terrible affair though.

August 30th

My last was sent off just as we had heard the unwelcome news of the loss of the *Northam*, and we started off an hour or two afterwards, hoping to be off the wreck on Saturday night. In consequence, however, of having to stop once or twice for hot bearings, we did not get to the Straits of Jubal before sunset, so were obliged to lie to for the night, and so lost nine or ten hours.

Every possible arrangement for the help of the unfortunate people on the reef was made, and the boats were all told off, each to have a certain quantity of food, water, arms, ammunition, etc. I volunteered for a boat, and was entrusted with the command of one of the life boats, the other boats being all under the command of the different officers, and the Purser going in charge of the mail boat. The Captain, one officer and four or five men, besides engineers, stokers, etc., being all who were to remain on board.

We made out the reef soon after daylight, but could make out no wreck; however, we got gradually closer, and it was just possible to make out some black mastless broken-up affair, which might possibly be the *Northam*, so the Chief Officer went in the gig to reconnoitre the Island where the passengers were known to have taken refuge, while the Third Officer was sent in another boat to look at the wreck. As the place was so full of reefs in every direction, it was not safe to venture in very far with the ship, especially as the pilot knew nothing really about the place, though he professed to be perfectly well acquainted with it.

There was no sign of any ship's boat, or of life at all, except in a number of Arab buggalows sailing from almost every direction towards us. We discovered a kind of flagstaff down by the water's edge of the Island, which proved to be the mast of a raft, and soon after the Chief Officer landed, he made the signal "Don't want the boats". Several buggalows now came alongside, all with provisions and water, and one with a letter from the British Consul at Djeddah to Capt. Stead, referring to a previous despatch,

89

and saying that he had sent divers, etc., etc. One buggalow brought two Lascars of the *Northam's* crew, who had been sent back from Suakin by Keatley and Algar with water, and we then made out another buggalow steering for us with evidently a ship's boat astern.

By and by the Chief Officer returned with a report that the Island was deserted; there were some remains of provisions and water there and he picked up a paper on which had been scrawled with a bit of charcoal "All safe, gone to Suez". This was so far satisfactory, but very indefinite, as they neither mentioned the date nor the vessel by which they were conveyed. Presently the buggalow came alongside with the *Northam's* mail boat in tow, which contained Keatley, the Admiralty Agent, and Algar the Purser, who had gone down to Serakin to telegraph the news, and back in this boat, a distance of about 120 miles each way. They were not at all sorry to get on board the *Benares*, but were equally surprised as ourselves to find the other birds flown. Soon after the Third Officer returned having inspected the whole of the reef without finding a single trace of the *Northam*, the wreck seen being only an old buggalow.[23]

We of course now can only conjecture what has become of the ship and passengers, and general opinion, in which Keatley and Algar join, is that the ship has slipped off and went in deep water as there was a depth of forty-five fathoms under the stern, and she was badly bilged and only on shore as far as the fore chain. I own that I am myself very hopeful that they have got her off and the passengers have gone on to Suez in her, for I know she is a strongly-built ship, and she seems to be perfectly tight except in the fore compartment. Then again, had they gone in another ship, they would surely have mentioned it in the paper left on the Island. However, you will know all about it before long. Before I do probably, or at any rate as soon.

It is consoling to know that they could not have been very badly off for either provisions or water, as they left some of both behind them. I shall be very anxious to know, for the *Northam* is a pet ship and a new one, so that the total loss would stand the Company in for nearly £100,000.

The Captain (Stead) is a great favourite of mine and withal a very nervous man, and I doubt if he would ever survive the loss of his vessel. Indeed, I should not be the least surprised to hear that this has been too much for him, even if the ship should eventually turn up all right. The Chief Officer, Sparkes, is one of the nicest fellows I ever met, and several of the passengers. The whole Matheson party came up with us in the *Benares* as far as The Mauritius. Considering the extra detention which the *Northam* had, I think she even beat the *Benares* up to Aden, but I have not had an

90

opportunity of looking over the logbook yet.

August 31st

Old Keatley does not seem to have suffered much from his exposure, though they must have gone through a great deal with the hot sun by day and intensely heavy dews at night. I expect he will get into a glorious row with his Lords Commissioners of the Admiralty for deserting his mails, which he had no more business to do than a Captain to leave his ship. The mails have gone on, how, when or where he does not know and the first request he made on reaching the quarter deck of the *Benares* was for Captain Scottowe to take him up to Suez at once. Cool, eh? It is my impression that he does not want to go up to Suez at all, but that he will endeavour to go down again as Admiralty Agent of the *Benares*, so as to let the affair blow over if possible before his return, when his time will be up and anyhow he will go on to England. I don't know, but it seems so to me from the fact that he overdoes his anxiety to get there.

For instance, last night the *Simla* passed us, bound to Suez. Directly she was sighted, old Keatley got into a fidget and said that he must go up by her and requested Captain Scottowe to speak to her. The Captain, willing to humour him and, I expect, not sorry at the idea of getting rid of him, stopped the ship, sounded the steam whistle, sent up rockets, burned blue lights, etc., etc., and the *Simla* bore down upon us and stopped within about a mile of us. A boat was lowered and all ready to start by the time *Simla* was stopped, but Keatley was nowhere to be found. At last he turned up, but then all his traps (the old fellow had saved everything from the *Northam*, not so many people) had to be put into the boat, then he must run over the other side of the ship and declare that the *Simla* was not near enough and that she should come in to within a quarter of a mile of us, and after all, he must remember that he had no cigars, and send down to the Chief Steward for some. By the time he got clear of the ship's side, the *Simla* had turned ahead again and would not stop any longer, so he had to come back pretending to be in a great rage and vowing that the P&O Company have no proper night signals, etc. I don't know what he would have better than rockets, blue lights and whistles. I believe that he has written an official letter to the Captain to know what the P&O night signals are, for the information of his Lords Commissioners of the Admiralty.

If I were Captain Scottowe, I think he should reply that I should be happy to afford any information to a person holding official authority to demand it, but that I must decline submitting the private arrangements of the

Company to general passengers, or something to that effect.

We have exchanged our Lascar crew for a European one shipped in Bombay, and the difference is wonderful. Our Lascar crew had got well accustomed to the ship and a finer set of men as a body were never mustered on the quarter-deck of any ship. The vessel was in magnificent condition and you might have eaten your dinner off any part of the deck. Now there is nothing but growling and quarrelling among the men themselves and a certain kind of slovenliness in the way of doing almost everything. They cannot work properly in this intense heat and they get discontented and dissatisfied. They were unable to get any Lascars to go down to Australia and so were obliged to send them, but I hope that e'er long they will be able to get regular Lascar crews for all the Australian ships.

September 1st

We arrived at Aden last night and received the welcome news that the *Northam* had been got off and had arrived safely at Suez on the 28th in time to catch her proper mail. This is indeed good news and I hope we shall get full particulars by the *Madras*.

I am very glad indeed to have got my present appointment at Singapore. I shall be a good deal more on my own responsibility there than in Bombay but, I think without boasting, I may say that I think myself well qualified for the post. Bombay is getting too full; there are too many in the office there now so that one is almost in as much a bundle of hay as in London, and from all accounts, Singapore is a delightful place with a very healthy climate. It will be a rising place as a Company's Station if we get a line to Japan and another to Siam from thence.

You may remember my mentioning that I had met in Melbourne an old schoolfellow who was dismissed for burglary.[24] It seems that the day after I saw him, he absconded from his employers with some £1,400 worth of jewellery and is supposed to have gone away to Rio on the *Oneida*. The hue and cry is after him all over the Colonies.

The *Simla* has brought shocking news from China.[25] The Admiral wounded and some 400 killed with four gunboats sunk and other damages to our gunboats, etc. In fact we seem to have got a decided thrashing somehow. I hope it will not be long before they will teach John Chinaman a good lesson for all this, otherwise the annoyance our people will have to suffer will be very great.

I am glad to say the *Northam* loss will not disarrange the Australian mail service as the *Malta* will be ready to take on the next mail. It is here that

P&O have an immense advantage over anyone else, in their great resources in case of emergencies of this nature.

September 10th, at Bombay
Just time to write one line to announce my safe arrival here last night after a splendid passage across in the *Madras*.[26]

September 27th
I wrote you a line from Bombay just after my arrival there. I was only a day or two in Bombay during which time I was as busy as I possibly could be so that I had hardly time to see anybody or to do anything except my P&O business.

I just saw Mrs. Townsend for a few minutes on three days. She is not looking very well, but that is not to be wondered at as everybody in Bombay seems to have been poorly lately. She has a person living with her whom I did not much admire, a Mrs. Nayer (or something of that sort); a decided chee-chee.

I left Bombay on the 16th September. We expect to get into Penang tomorrow morning. I went on shore at Galle and was very much pleased indeed with the place. It is very different to Bombay and seems clean and sweet, reminding one more of Mauritius.

At Galle, we took on board a number of passengers so as to fill every berth in the ship. They were nearly all French, Dutch or Spanish, so that their jargon and dirt may be better imagined than described. Mine was a two-berth cabin and my companion a Spaniard, the Solicitor-General at Manila, who could not speak a word of English, and his French was considerably worse than mine, but between Spanish, French, English, Hindustani and fingers, we managed to make each other understand pretty fairly. There was one advantage about him, he only used the washing basin once a day for a minute or two, so that I had that pretty well to myself and I was not troubled with him much at night as I had secured the top berth, just under the port, and the bottom one has not much air so that he generally slept outside as did a great many others.

Talk about eating among Englishmen, to see the quantities and variety which these fellows put down would astonish one of our turtle-eating Aldermen. Hot roast pork, currant jelly, herrings and marmalade all on the same plate and going down together, helped down by half a pint of salad oil! Eugh!

Then their dress. The man I was with, I know did not take his trousers off from the time he entered the ship till the time I left it. All day and all night the same brown woollen hot-looking clothes, and he used to look quite astonished at me when he saw me put on a clean pair of white trousers every morning and sleep in pyjamas.

September 28th

Arrived at Penang. Went on shore for a stroll. There is a very pretty waterfall which I went to have a look at and I also walked through the native bazaar which is very much cleaner than Bombay, though their inhabitants are nearly all Chinese who are proverbially dirty in their habits.

NOTES

1. This is possibly Kendall's own sailing boat at Portsmouth.

2. See entry for July 12th.

3. P&O's early uniforms were so similar to those of the Royal Navy that, in 1846, they were asked by the Admiralty to modify them.

4. Probably a reference to the French promise to the Sardinians to support them with 200,000 men in a war with Austria.

5. Sir John Lawrence was Chief Commissioner of the Punjab Province and quelled the riots at Meerut and Delhi for which he was given a baronetcy and the GCB. He returned home to England in 1859 as a member of the Secretary of State's Council until 1864 when he returned to India as Viceroy and Governor-General.

6. Arthur Anderson was one of the founders of the P&O Company and was Managing Director at this time. He became Chairman in 1862 following the death of Willcox, a position he held until his own death in February 1868, aged 77. He is likely to have been in Egypt for discussions on the Suez Canal project.

7. Capt. Robert Methven joined P&O in 1851, having served his time in sail, and within two years (at the age of 37) was promoted to Commander. He wrote a book, "The Log of a Merchant Officer", in an attempt to improve the training and status of seafarers. In 1860, he was removed from the service in consequence of being in general disagreement with the Managing Director's orders but reinstated the following year. He continued in command until his retirement at the age of 65.

8. The Company's Regulations issued to Pursers and Clerks-in-Charge in 1860 included the following:-

> In your intercourse with Passengers you will be required to exercise patience, forbearance and good temper.
> Do not on any account permit eating and drinking to take place on deck, or elsewhere in the saloon, except by the Surgeon's order.
> You must be particularly vigilant...on your morning round that the livestock is properly fed and attended to, that the water closets are in a proper state, and the tanks filled.

9. Bugle calls were for many years, even until the 1960's, the recognised manner of announcing meals on board P&O, B.I. and Orient Line ships.

10. P&O included all liquors in its fares which sometimes led to requests for refunds from teetotallers. For this reason, Pursers were forbidden to give teetotal passengers Certificates of Abstinence.

11. The *Sarah Sands* was a vessel carrying troops from Cape Town to India which caught fire. The damage sustained caused the vessel to drop anchor in Port Louis harbour where repairs were undertaken. It was evidently something of a tourist attraction while there.

12. When Mauritius was ceded to the British in 1814, the latter agreed to maintain French law and customs. Thus, although Mauritius was a British colony until 1964, it maintained its French way of life. The tomb of Paul and Virginia is situated in the garden of Pamplemousses, about eight miles from Port Louis.

13. As far as we know, Kendall did not wear spectacles and it is likely that the goggles referred to were tinted glasses.

14. *Dunbar* was a ship of 1,321 tons which was wrecked in bad weather on South Head at the entrance to Sydney harbour on the night of 20 August, 1857. Of the 122 people on board, only one was saved.

15. At this time, P&O were using Government facilities for drydocking their ships. In this case, *Benares* was in for routine drydocking and for alterations to the pitch of the propellers.

16. Kendall had possibly noticed convict labour being used in the Portsmouth Dockyards.

17. Kendall returned to Australia in 1865 and worked for many years in Melbourne.

18. Since Kendall left Mauritius on 9 July, he would have been unaware of the Armistice concluded the previous day at Villafranca following some appalling battles in which the Austrians lost 22,000 men and the Allies 17,000. Under the terms of the Armistice, Austria ceded Lombardy while Napoleon received Savoy and Nice from Sardinia.

19. The new Government was that of the second Liberal administration of Palmerston. Nicholas Kendall ('The Squire' and a cousin of Franklin) of Pelyn was returned as one of the members for the eastern division of Cornwall. Mr. Waguelin was one of the Directors of P&O.

20. Testimony of the Rocks, published in 1857, is subtitled "Geology in its bearings on the two theologies, natural and revealed".

21. In 1811, Mehmet Ali invited all the Mameluke chiefs then in Cairo to a ceremony in the palace. After welcoming them, heavy fire was directed on them from above and behind. One Mameluke only survived by jumping 164 feet (St. Paul's is 365 feet high) from the top of the Citadel on his horse. The massacre was the signal for the indiscriminate slaughter of the Mamelukes throughout Egypt.

22. In computers, glass and gold are used as insulators and conductors respectively.

23. The early days of sea travel could, of course, be hazardous and Kendall's description gives a good indication of the organisation that could be swiftly brought to bear by P&O in cases of accident.

24. See entry for June 17th.

25. In June 1859 when envoys came to exchange the ratification of treaties with China and to take up residence in Pekin, they found the road blocked. A Chinese escort was provided to conduct the envoys by way of a port used by the bearers of tribute by subject states. The American envoy chose to go by the suggested route, the Russians by another route; neither gained much in dignity. The British and French, however, attempted to force their way past the Taku forts and were repulsed.

26. It is likely that Kendall travelled to Aden in *Benares* and then transferred to *Madras* for the journey to Singapore via Bombay.

5 The P&O's new ship *Poonah*, 1863

6

At Singapore

September 30th, 1859

Arrived at Singapore and was met on board by Jellicoe. It is a beautiful place, and if I can only get enough to live upon here, I am sure I shall be in clover.

An English shilling equals a Bombay rupee equals a Singapore dollar, so that expenses are necessarily heavy, and as the Company pay the rent of the house in which Jellicoe and I live, I shall not be able to draw house rent allowance, so that in point of fact, I shall be £50 a year poorer than when I first went to Bombay, with a more responsible position and double the expenses.

This is looked upon as the Company's best station in the East, and truly it is a beautiful place; there is also a fives ground and cricket club, with good shooting near, and a glorious place for a shady swim just at the bottom of our garden, with no fear of sharks or sunstroke or any other abominations to deter one from enjoying it. The P&O dockyards here are acknowledged to be the best-kept and neatest place of any kind in the East, and I may say I think in the world. There is no dry dock, but works, carpenters, blacksmiths, etc., etc., shops, and coal sheds, all as clean and neat as a new pin, and I can only say that as far as I have anything to do with it, I will endeavour to keep up the reputation which it has earned, and which may be done at very little expense to the Company. I have been enough among ships and dockyards now to know a ringbolt from a cow's tail, so I have no doubt I shall manage and I shall be at the same time learning myself.

October 6th

There is one great advantage here over Bombay and almost every other port I have been in. It is a free port and there is no bother with the Custom House, which is always one of the most disagreeable parts of one's business and is a great additional expense.

It is very hot here in the middle of the day, but in the morning and evening it is deliciously cool. I have got such a glorious bath, I can sit in it up to my neck in water and it is so delicious. It has a showerbath fitted over the top so that I get such a splendid bath each morning, it is worth the voyage out here to try it almost.

I think if I had been going over to Canada about the same time as dear Edward,[1] I would have taken passage in the *Great Eastern*.[2] I would give something to make the first voyage in her.

November 3rd

It is the fashion here to go out calling on people whether one has an introduction or not and so, directly after the last mail had gone, I went out with Jellicoe for a day or two to introduce myself.

The first person I called on was a Mrs. Van Hoorne, a Dutch lady who is famous for her crinolines, the wife of a merchant, an agreeable and rather nice-looking woman, and then we went to a Mrs. Harrison, another merchant's wife, a chatty individual. I also called on Mrs. Rigg, the wife of the Commissioner of Police, a Mrs. Campbell who was not at home or ill or something, and on the Padre. He, the latter, is a very agreeable man; his name is Smyth. Then another day we had tiffin with Mrs. D'Almeida, the wife of a Portuguese (pukkah, not Indian) millionaire. She herself is an Englishwoman and I liked her very much, but she has the peculiar failing which most ladies in a small community seem to indulge in of dearly loving a little gossip.

Another day I called on Mrs. Burne, the wife of General Burne, the Brigadier commanding here, a very jolly person with an unmarried daughter whose present name is decidedly the most appropriate she could have as her hair is a very decidedly auburn, or as uncharitable people might say, but never mind what uncharitable people might say, we won't. The Brigadier, or as he is generally termed, Briggs, returned my visit yesterday. Then I called on Mrs. McNaer, the wife of a Captain in the Artillery, a large quiet person, and Mrs. Armstrong, an old widow lady who delights in large bonnets and limp skirts, and who has a very pretty laughing-eyed daughter, the Belle of the place, and three huge sons, all over six feet and stout and strong in proportion.

I suppose I ought to have begun with Government House, but I thought it better not to call there just at first as Colonel Cavenagh was away. I called the day after he returned and found his wife a particularly nice person. I did not see him, of course. He is rather a little man, shortsighted and with a wooden leg, and she is a fine tall well-made person.

November 5th

As expected, I am up to my eyes in work. It is worse than I expected as the *Norna* made a provokingly quick run and got in yesterday. The *Ottawa* only arrived this morning, so I have had all the bother of rewriting and altering the official letters, adding PS's, etc., etc., etc., etc., etc., and all to do in one or two hours.

November 14th

I don't know whether I have yet given you a description of our house. It is a nice large airy bungalow built, as is usual here, on small pillars about five feet high to keep off ants, etc., etc. It stands on top of a small hill, which runs out into New Harbour, so that we are bounded by the sea on three sides, and have a most magnificent view and all the cool breezes.

The scenery all round New Harbour is very pretty, reminding me not a little of Sydney in miniature, as there are one or two deepwater bays running out of it on both sides, which look very pretty. We can also see ships coming in from both south and west almost as soon as they can from the signal staff.[3]

The house consists of a large drawing room in front, with an immense verandah at one end, and a small room in front, with two good-sized bedrooms each with washing room, dressing room, and a bathroom attached, and a dining room at the back. There is also a small detached bungalow in which a man named Simson, who lives with us, sleeps, and as we shall want a spare room, we are having another similar bungalow built, so that altogether we have a very nice comfortable house, of which the Company of course pays the rent.

The landlord is the Tumongong or native rajah to whom the whole of this place formerly belonged, and he and his two sons are very agreeable, intelligent men. The two sons both came up to call upon me soon after I came, and I often go to have a game of bowls with them.

We have only to pull across, or walk round a small bay, to be in the P&O Dockyard, and either Jellicoe or I generally go over of a morning before breakfast. We have a very nice garden, with a nice little private landing place, with good stables, cowhouses, fowlhouses, pigeon house, pig pens, etc., etc., etc., so that we are pretty well off as regards quarters, and I think we are likely to harmonise very well together, as both Jellicoe and Simson are very nice fellows, and I think we are all three well suited to one another. Simson is in a merchant's house here, the largest and oldest I think in the place.

There are a great many Chinese in Singapore and nearly everyone has a Chinaman for a servant.

People seem very sociable and friendly here and there is none of that abominable clique system of Bombay or Calcutta. I had a call from Padre Smyth the other day. He, as well as most people here, is an enthusiastic Mason and I suppose they will be persuading me to join them some day, though I don't just yet as I can't afford it.[4]

Almost everyone here goes by some nickname or other. I have been christened Gibbons; why, I don't know, except that I believe I am supposed to be like an individual of that name who used to be here.

I think I told you in my last that my pugga has been increased to $150 a month, or at Company's rate of exchange £375 a year. This is actually of not much more value, I think, than my pay in Bombay, as expenses here are a good deal heavier, but I think it is enough for me to live on and I am quite satisfied. In another month or two I shall see how it works, and then I hope that I may be able to increase my remittances a little, but I do not like to promise till I know how I am off. It is a better place to remit from than Bombay, as the Company pay at a fixed rate of 4/2d per $, and the Banks will generally give from 4/6d to 4/7d at sight in London so that in remitting £5 I gain nearly 10/- while at Bombay I could never get more than par.

The *Bahiana* came in on the tenth with the Electric Cable from hence to Batavia. She was consigned to us, and lay alongside our wharf, so that I had several opportunities of going over her. It has been quite a gala time for Singapore, and the quantity of cold ham and champagne consumed on board during the few days she was here must have been considerable. There seems to be perpetual tiffin going on, as visitors come at all hours of the day, and Mr. Gordon, the Managing Partner of Messrs. Newall and Co., who has come out to superintend the laying of the cable, is such a thoroughly agreeable man, that I think all the ladies lost their hearts to him. The cable appears to be beautifully made and coiled and the apparatus for paying it out is so simple and at the same time so ingenious that I think a fracture is almost impossible while paying out, unless from some defect in the cable. She commenced paying out yesterday morning (Nov. 15th) and hitherto all has gone well. They hope to have it completed to Batavia in a week.

Everybody here has been very much interested in the *Great Western*.[5] The explosion on board seems to have been a terrible affair, but I am hardly surprised at it. I hope that now they have had lesson enough and will be a little more careful next time.

The tidings of the return of McClintock's expedition and the news of poor Uncle Franklin's death have, of course, been of very great interest.[6] It must be far better for poor Lady Franklin to know that her husband was so early relieved from those frightful sufferings which the others must have undergone. The nation should indeed drop a tear to the memory of that brave handful of its sons who have fallen martyrs in the cause of science and accord all honours to those who by dint of untiring exertions have brought to light in a few months, with a small yacht, what several large expeditions have in the course of years failed to accomplish. The least they should do to McClintock would be, I think, to accord the same honour to him as to McLure.[7]

November 18th

I am so glad to get the two books and the paint box belonging to dearest Mary. How it constantly reminds one of the dear departed to handle her own books, with her own marks in her own handwriting. It seems a connecting link between the irrevocable past, the visible present and the incomprehensible future, and in every page which I read I shall see, as it were, dear Mary's face reflected.

> *Or often as we pause and look*
> *Where in some daily handled book*
> *Approval's well known tokens stand,*
> *Traced by some dear familiar hand.*

November 21st

Townsend has got the Company's storeship *Fort William* at Hong Kong, so I hope they will be pretty comfortable there.

December 5th

My beautiful boy leaves me today. He is such a tremendous thickhead that I can't stand him any longer, and his place is to be supplied by a native of Pondicherry, an accomplished gentleman who can speak French, Hindustani, Malay and a little English. I expect he will be a great rogue, as these accomplished individuals nearly always are, but he brings good recommendations and I can but try him for a while.

Our Chaplain, Mr. Smyth, is by far the best specimen of an Indian clergyman I have ever seen. He is a thoroughly good man, very agreeable, and very clever, and has the most wonderful memory I ever met with. He preaches always extemporary, but the most laboured written sermon could not be more eloquent with less repetition and to the point and we are most fortunate in having such an excellent good man.

The Bishop of Labuan has been here some little time, on his way to England.[8] He is a clever man I think, and a very agreeable person to talk to, but is not very episcopal-looking. He dresses more like a Jewish Rabbi or Romish Priest than an English Bishop, and looks as if he had been a good many years in the country as he is thoroughly bronzed. He wears a long black beard and moustache and the expression of his countenance is thoroughly good-natured. He reminds me, in fact, a little of Uncle Henry.

It remains to be seen how the policy will work with Indian finance.[9] I confess that I am not very sanguine. I think he knows too much of English statistics and the mode of carrying on the treasury business in England to be able to enter into the spirit of Indian Government, and they cannot be conducted in the same way. We have gone a great deal too far, as it is, with the "Liberal English Policy"; it does not at all suit the disposition of the native subjects, and we shall find that out some day to our cost. He is notoriously a "Free Trade" man, and I am afraid that he will be introducing all sorts of experiments which will probably prove signal failures and which would not be thought of by a man well acquainted with the Indian character.

He came out with Weston in the *Nemesis* and I believe that they were not altogether very comfortable on board. The ship is about the most uncomfortable one in the service, they were very crowded and had rather disagreeable weather, besides which Weston is a man who will have his own way on board his own ship, and is therefore not always very popular with passengers. For instance, he holds a theory, I think a very correct one, that the mail service should be considered as a service and not with respect to his own particular ship, so that if he commands the fastest ship on the line, he will not, for the sake of getting a name for the vessel, drive her to make a wonderful passage, but will stick to his contract time, or at most one day before, so that if by means of a good breeze he finds himself well ahead, he will ease down and save his fuel, rather than run on at once, and make a passage. This of course passengers don't like, but where there are two or three junctions on a line, I think that punctuality should be kept to, as much as on a railway. You never hear of a London train reaching Bishopstoke en route for Portsmouth a quarter of an hour before its time, neither should you hear of the Calcutta steamer having arrived at Galle five or six days before her time. People grumble if others don't, and you will see long articles in Calcutta papers anathematising the P&O for not putting faster steamers on the line. The "So and So" arrived in so many days, why shouldn't all the ships do it in the same time?", etc., etc., etc.

During the voyage out of the *Nemesis* it seems that for two or three days it had been found necessary to close all the ports. This of course made it hot and uncomfortable, but it couldn't be avoided; if anyone surreptitiously opened the port he was punished for it by getting well drenched. One day, it was thought proper to close the stern ports and, as people didn't like that, they went and opened them, risking a ducking. Weston, when he saw that the ports had been opened contrary to orders, turned astern and literally flooded the saloon with water, to the great disgust of people who were there reading or writing, etc.

I had a letter from Uncle Henry some little time ago. Of Alfred he says, "I shall say nothing about the young man further than I think it was a confounded mistake his ever getting possession of such a girl as Mary."

The "Illustrated News", with the pictures and accounts of McClintock's expedition, has been most interesting. How touching to receive back a letter written eleven years before. Poor Uncle Franklin, but he had been called hence even before that letter was commenced.

December 20th, 1859

The Bishop of Labuan has been here lately and left only the other day in the *Bahiana*. It was very interesting to see him administer the Holy Communion to native converts in the native language. The usual plan is to have an interpreter who translates each sentence after the clergyman. I also witnessed the Christening of a Chinese moonshee, named Ling Chong See, the other day. Here the man could not speak a word of English, as none of the Chinese here except a few can, and the Padre cannot speak Malay, so the Interpreter was called in requisition.

There is an anecdote told of the Bishop of Labuan which so corresponds with the general manner of the man that I feel sure it must be true. It seems that a small steamer was going up a river there, wanting a pilot, and it so happened that the Bishop, a dark unshorn odd-looking man, was in the boat by himself fishing, and being dressed in old clothes they mistook him for a pilot, and the following dialogue took place: "Boat ahoy!" "Aye, aye." "Are you a pilot?" "No, I'm the Bishop, but I'll pilot you if you like. Heave us a rope", and he accordingly jumped on board and took the vessel up to port.

What a dreadful thing the wreck of the *Royal Charter* is! [10] A splendid ship as she was, and with so many on board, suddenly and without warning almost doomed to a water grave, when so nearly at the end of their journey. It is even worse than the unfortunate *Dunbar* at Sydney.

Talk about Australia being full of Scotchmen, what would anybody say of Singapore? Jellicoe and I are almost the only two Englishmen in the place, the rest being with very few exceptions about 75% Scotch and 25%

103

Germans. As there are a good many Yankee ships frequenting the port, there is a small sprinkling of Yankees, and I was rather amused the other day by hearing a man ask a native if he could speak American, not condescending, of course, to call it English.

It is coming on towards Christmas time now but does not seem like Christmas a bit, and yet it seems three or four years ago since I spent my last Christmas Day at Bandra with the Mattheys. I don't suppose I shall dine out on Christmas Day this year as, although I have several acquaintants here, I have not yet any such intimate friends as they were.

January 21st, 1861 [11]

I can assure you my heart was in more than one place in England on Xmas Day, when I thought of old times, old friends and familiar faces.

No-one here seems to take an interest in Christmas somehow, nearly everyone is Scotch, and the Scotch always exclude Christmas and think of nothing but the New Year. There is nothing to remind one of the season at all. Even in church, we had but one hurried service on Christmas morning, with no Communions, and there has been no service since, except on Sunday, not even on New Year's Day, and scarcely any allusion whatever to the season in Mr. Nicholson's sermons. He said that he understood it was not usual to have Communion on Christmas Day or services on any other day but Sunday. I do not know who could have told him so, for Mr. Smyth invariably had, and always used to take notice in his sermons of the seasons as we passed through them.

We have had very little gaiety at all. In fact, there are not many such things as Christmas parties given in this part of the world but there is to be a big dance at Mrs. Jose D'Almeida's the day after tomorrow.

Before this reaches you, I shall probably be one of the Free and Accepted Craftsmen of the Eastern Archipelago, having been proposed as a member of the Lodge by the Provincial Grand Secretary, Jellicoe, and seconded by the Worshipful Provincial Grand Master, Simon.

It is a great mistake to think that I am getting fatter. I do not know that I am much thinner, but I have lost in weight considerably since I came to Singapore. I am sure too, if you saw me after a three hours' game of bowls, which I very often play, you wouldn't say that I did not take exercise, and did you see the modest wing of fowl or slice of mutton with bread and cheese and a glass of beer, which is my usual dinner, you would not say that I lived particularly luxuriously.

The Chinese New Year is just coming on, when we may look for a few rows among them. They appear to have been rather incensed by the policemen lately, and yesterday several reports were rife of policemen having been murdered at some of the out-stations, and several more threatened. One report is confirmed but the others are I hope not true, but a considerable force has been sent to Budu, the scene of the murder, for the purpose of reclaiming a policeman who is said to have been carried away into the jungle.[12] If there is much more of it, I think it very probable that the Volunteers will be called out, as they have been more than once before on similar occasions. It is well known that any number of Chinamen cannot stand against a very few disciplined men with bayonets, and they generally only require a demonstration, so if it should be found necessary to resort to extreme measures there is not likely to be any actual fighting.

Sinclair sent me one of the new bronze pennies. They are much lighter and more portable than the old coppers, but I don't very much admire the coinage and I should fancy the impressions would wear out very soon. I see there is quite a discussion in the papers about them.[13]

February 21st

I am beginning my letter under decided difficulties. The rain is pelting down in torrents and, although quite late enough to be daylight, it is almost as dark as when I went to bed last night. Altogether one of those particularly depressing days when, as Punch says, the only thing to be done is to look out of windows and strop razors.

We had quite an acquisition to Singapore society by last mail: Lady McCausland and her daughter, a blooming young Irish lassie of seventeen or eighteen years, and Miss Cowper, the daughter of the Resident Surgeon who came out under Lady McCausland's chaperonage, if there is such a word.

On Monday morning, just after daylight, as I was deliberating with myself whether I should get up or take forty winks more, I heard someone come into my house and along the passage past my bedroom, singing out, "Anybody at home?" I jumped up and caught a glimpse of a man whom I thought at first a stranger but almost immediately recognised. "Townsend, by Jove!" I exclaimed, and sure enough there was the gallant Commander of the *Shanghai*. The ship, you must know, is under charter to the French Government and has been sent down from Shanghai to Saigon, from whence she was suddenly ordered on here and came in unexpectedly on Sunday evening. Mrs. Townsend, having obtained leave from the French Admiral, has been cruising about with her husband for some time past, and so we have now the pleasure of her company for a few days, till the *Shanghai* leaves again, which will probably be on Sunday or Monday next. The ship is entirely under the orders of the French Government, so that we have nothing whatever to do with her, except to look after any stores and repairs which she may require. She flies the French pennant and French ensign, which I don't think she has any business to, and discards the humble bunting of the P&O Company.

There have been three Russian men-of-war here for the last three weeks on their way from Shanghai to Cronstadt and as a natural consequence we are inundated with Russian sailors. They, however, behave pretty well and are not nearly such a nuisance as English sailors would be in a foreign town. I believe they are to sail in about a week, calling at Batavia on their way to Europe.

On Saturday evening last, there were two or three smart shocks of an earthquake distinctly felt over nearly the whole of Singapore. We at New Harbour did not perceive it, but at the other side of the City, in the direction of Tanglin, it seems to have been very severe: bottles were thrown down off tables, doors began banging, lamps dancing, etc., etc. I have heard that two Chinese houses were thrown down but this I cannot vouch for, the other I know to be true. The natives were running about the streets in a state of great excitement, not knowing what to make of it. Such an event rarely occurs in Singapore, though it is not so uncommon in Java. The natives are beginning to attribute it to the Telegraphic Cable laid between this and Batavia, although it is not in working order at present.

February 22nd

It has just ceased raining for the first time since the day before yesterday. Yesterday was one of the worst days I ever saw in any part of the world: the rain was so thick that it was almost impossible to see across the street. A French steamer started for Saigon but, thinking discretion the better part of valour, came back again before she got to the lighthouse. The Dutch steamers could not get in from Batavia, and the *Madras* with the mails arrived off port the evening before and could not get in till eight o'clock yesterday evening. Some walls and masonry posts have been literally washed away in our neighbourhood by the rain and our old house leaks like a sieve. The roads are in a frightful state which will be a fruitful source of bullying for Jellicoe who is one of the newly elected Municipal Commissioners.

I see that the Emperor of the French has abolished passports through

France for English subjects, so he really does seem as if he meant reform. I am very glad of it, as far as we are concerned, as it will save us a great deal of trouble in seeing that passengers have their passports properly visaed before they embark, which we had to do under the old system.[14]

People may call the P&O what they like, but no-one in England has any idea of the expenses of steamers in this part of the world. They compare our rates with Cunard's, and say "Look at the difference", so say I, "Look at the difference". Cunard is paid about 13/- per mile for running the mails (Royal Mail's are 9/10d and P&O 4/6d). Cunard coals cost him on average 12/- per ton, P&O coals in the East average £3.0.0 to £3.5.0. Hams and cheeses, jams, wines, beer, etc., etc., and all kinds of Purser's stores are not bought out in the East, or sent out to the East for what they cost at home. Wages are higher, repairs are higher, and everything is higher, very considerable, so that I believe, taking all in all, as compared with other steamer lines, the P&O will be found as cheap, if not cheaper, than any other.

As regards the treatment on board, you will never find people on board ship who do not growl at something whether they have occasion to or not. They have nothing else to do. 999 complaints out of every thousand are frivolous and not worth answering; the remaining one is generally an unavoidable one, from some accidental cause which the Company could not control.

Macaulay is going down to Australia for a cruise to recruit his health.

There appears to be some likelihood of a disturbance at Japan, but I hope it may turn out all right.[15]

March 8th

We have been having wonderful weather here. All the time the Townsends were with us, it was raining cats and dogs. We have had another shock of an earthquake the last fortnight and a few days ago a large waterspout passed along the harbour within a hundred yards of the office. It has been something terrific in the China Sea; ships have been putting back dismasted and damaged in all sorts of ways, and the old *Pekin* with Mr. Ritchie on board got a great hammering going up the China Sea.

The other night, we were dining out at the McTaggerts' and slept at Murray's in the neighbourhood as it was so long a drive home. On getting to the office in the morning the Peon came and reported that the old Butler had been taking a considerable quantity of our brandy and treating some of his friends, and that at seven o'clock in the evening he ordered out Jellicoe's buggy, and one of the ponies. He then got into it with four of his friends and went to Singapore, driving all about the place and returning at one a.m. He then took another pony and remained out till five the next morning. This was rather too much and Jellicoe, having ascertained that he could get no redress at the Police, discharged him at once without his pay, a month's wages due. I have not seen him since, as he has kept out of my way, but I don't think he was half punished enough, and I shall make him feel the weight of my whip, as he did my pony, if I catch hold of him. I think it is about the most impudent thing I have heard of for a long while. It so happened that the pony which he worked most was sick, and under a course of physic. We were not using him ourselves, and had he taken some physic which he ought to have had that day, the work would probably have killed him. This is a specimen of what our servants are when we have not our eyes exactly upon them.

I am afraid next mail will bring serious news from America.[16] I do not like the look of things there at all. All the Americans abroad are, I think, adverse to fighting and I hope the good sense of the people at home will keep them quiet. If the cotton supply is stopped, I can't imagine what England would do for, although people have been energetic lately in getting up all sorts of schemes for growing cotton in Africa, India, Australia, etc., they cannot do it all at once, and the supply from America which should have to be made up is almost immense.

The Chambers left us yesterday in Sir John Brooke's little vessel the *Rainbow* for Sarawak. The *Rainbow* is a nice little steamer, and as she is going to run regularly and only takes two or three days to cross, I think it very likely I shall take a run over to Sarawak one of these days.

March 23rd

Sinclair sent me a very nice little portrait of himself done on card. I am so pleased with it that I am going to ask both you and Edward if you will mind having yours done like it and sent out to me. Your large portrait has faded so much that it bears now but little resemblance to you, and Mrs. Townsend when she was here wanted to take it down from my dressing table as it gave such a wrong impression of you. I have no portrait of Edward as a clergyman and, when one is exiled from home and all dear ones, it is such a pleasure to be able to look upon the dear familiar faces on paper.

The accident on the South Western Railway seems to have been a terrible affair, and moreso as they are apparently unable to discover any cause of it. I know well the horrors of a railway accident and shall never forget that Sunday night that I spent at Lee among mangled dead and dying people who

108

had been well and hearty ten minutes before.[17]

Owing to a paltry dispute with the Post Office Authorities, in which we had undoubted right on our side, but which our people foolishly, I think, chose to compromise, we have been compelled to keep up two coaling establishments at Singapore, about three miles distance from one another. Now our New Harbour coal is the finest and most complete establishment of the kind in the world, and quite as much as we shall ever want; besides, our contract with the Government distinctly states that the vessels are all to go into New Harbour, yet for years we have had to keep up another coal wharf and send coals out by boats to all the outward steamers, which lie in the outer roads. This is now to be all done away with, and in addition to the immense sum saved to the Company, and the greater convenience of landing and shipping passengers and cargo alongside a wharf, we shall gain about an hour and a half in the receipt of letters, a great desideratum. The Post Office people have not opposed the movement in any way; in fact, they have quite been willing to co-operate with us in everything.

It is rather curious but at the same time that the whole of the Netherlands almost have been under water, there has been a terrible inundation in the Dutch Settlements in Java which has caused the destruction of a great deal of life and property.[18]

May 6th

One line, my dearest mother, just to say that I am all well, and that I have your letter of March 19th which shall be answered by next mail.

The *Formosa* came in on Friday and leaves this morning for Saigon. I made up my mind, if possible, to get a run up on her, but was afraid I should be unable to as she was going back again so soon. By dint of working very hard, however, I have just managed to get my work sufficiently well up to say at the last minute that I will go.

May 12th, at Saigon

I have not yet had an opportunity of seeing the "Essays and Reviews" which are so much in everyone's mouth just now, but I must try and get them to read over with the critiques and refutations of them in the "Guardian" and elsewhere. I see that Doctor Temple claims an individuality for his essays on the ground that they were preached some years ago before the University of Oxford without exciting remark, and that he has nothing to do with the opinions of others whose writings are in the same book. It is a pity, however, that he did not find out what these opinions were before allowing them to be published in the same book with them, thereby identifying himself to a great extent with them.[19]

I cannot help thinking what a blackguard that Major Yelverton must have been.[20] I read the report of his trial the other day and am very glad to see that his first wife has obtained her rights, though there is no doubt that she behaved foolishly to him before their marriage. Poor Mrs. Forbes and her children, one cannot but feel very much, there will be so much public sympathy with her that her misfortune will perhaps not be so much felt in this generation as in her children's and grandchildren's.

You will want to be hearing of my trip and so I will begin from the morning when I wrote my last.

Having made up my mind that I would not lose this opportunity, which was the best and indeed only one which I was likely to have, I lost no time in getting my boy to put a few clothes together. Then went to the French Consul from whom I got a passport, "Au nom de l'Empereur", especially recommending me to the kind care and attention of the civil and military officers of the port of Saigon, and also an order for passage in the *Formosa*.

We started about noon and nothing particular occurred on the way up. After a very pleasant and rather rapid passage of less than three days, we arrived off Cape St. James about nine o'clock on the morning of the ninth.

There is a large French frigate stationed off the mouth of the river, under the lee of the Cape, as a guard ship. We stopped and delivered letters to her and then steamed on up the river which is, I suppose, one of the most wonderful rivers in the world. Except at the entrance, it is nowhere very wide but, I suppose, averages the width of the Thames at Woolwich. It is very winding and the scenery along its banks is rather pretty, though there is a great deal of sameness about it from its being so flat. It is almost a level plain extending, I suppose, for some hundreds of miles, and yet close alongside the banks of the river there is deep water the whole way up, except in one or two places where there are sandbanks.

Saigon lies about sixty or sixty-five miles up the river and, having a strong tide in our favour, we got up there about half past two. The harbour, or rather reach (for the river is no wider here than anywhere else), is full of ships, mostly French transports, coal ships and gunboats, and there are also a few English and other vessels loading rice.

We had to turn round to go alongside a coalship and, in doing so, went so far astern that we nearly knocked over a tree on the river bank with our stern, nearly touching bottom, though we were sweeping the bushes in every direction.

The *Shanghai* was the other side of the coal ship and one of the first things which I did was to go over and rejoice poor Captain Townsend's heart by the confirmation of the news of his appointment to the hulk, of which he had heard vague rumours but nothing else and of which he has even now received no official news.

Saigon itself is a miserable place, but I will venture to say that under English rule it would in a very few years be one of the largest and richest trading ports in the East. Its natural advantages as a port are immense from the great depth of water in the river, and there is an unlimited supply of rice which can be cheaply and expeditiously brought down to the town from all parts of the neighbouring country in boats.

The French, however, do not understand what they are doing at all and they own it themselves that if we had the place we should make a great deal more of it. They seem to delight in harassing and annoying the natives as much as they can. They knock down their houses, burn their rice, make them work like so many convicts chained together, when they catch them, and stop all their trade. Their only idea is "La Gloire", and the capture of one or two small junks or topes which they may catch breaking the blockade is paraded in an official despatch as a "glorious engagement" and the capture of so many valuable "prizes". Then again, they don't look after their men at all; they make them work in the sun without awnings, lie down on the damp ground without tents, pay them very badly and feed them worse. What wonder then that they die off like sheep, that officers and men get discontented and disheartened, that discipline is slackened and that they are detested by the natives of the country. What would be thought on board an English man-of-war of a man heaving the lead under the Captain's nose, with no shirt on? Of sailors coming aft on the quarter-deck abusing the officers and smoking and spitting all about the place?

The way too in which business is mismanaged and the public money squandered is so patent to any sound-thinking man, that were one-fiftieth part of the waste to take place in any English-ruled settlement, the public press would be up in arms at once. I do not mean to say that we English are by any means immaculate, but we have a semblance at any rate of management and order in the way we do things, which Johnny Crapaud has not.

To give you some idea of the immense expense to which they are unnecessarily put through mismanagement, I may mention that there is a large fleet of vessels in the river, with coals for the Government. These vessels have mostly been lying there for several months and their charter

111

time has expired long ago, so that the French are paying about £50 sterling per day per ship for demurrage, taking the coal slowly away in driblets from two ships at a time by sending steamers alongside to coal. This they do although they have large lighters and every facility for landing or transferring coals from one ship to another, but they don't think of it.

Then again, in the ruined forts and houses of the place are thousands upon thousands of the most magnificent bricks in the world, and yet they fill our ships in Singapore with tons of the worst description of native brick for which they pay a high price, and on the ships' arrival in Saigon bundle them out onto the beach where they are all broken up in a day or two and never used.

But I daresay you will have had enough of French politics and mismanagement and will like to hear something more of the place and how I spent my time. The scenery along all the rivers is much the same, flat but pretty from the number and variety of the trees which grow down to the water's edge and are full of birds, monkeys, etc., etc.

There is very little to notice in the actual town of Saigon, except the cleanliness and good order of all the parts where the mercenary Manila troops or "Tagals" are quartered, and the discomfort and filth of most places where the French are.[21] The "Town", as it is called by courtesy, consists of a few straggling houses all of one storey only; streets, properly so called, there are none and the shops are small and badly supplied. The only chance to buy provisions is to get up early in the morning and go to the market which is supplied then with meat, fish, poultry, vegetables, fruit, etc.

The principal part of the business is transacted in the "CHINA CITY!" which is about four miles from Saigon proper, up a very pretty creek. There is a large quantity of rice continually coming, and in spite of the discouragement which the French give to all kinds of business, Chinamen will trade. I dined one night with Behre and Kufeke, the partners in the German house. We sat down to a capital dinner and had a splendid lobster salad, such as I had not tasted since I left England. Crabs, lobsters, shrimps and prawns abound in Saigon and are very good.

One day I pulled up to the China Town but beyond the scenery of the river, and a magnificent joss house which they have, there was nothing different to any other Chinese place of business; indeed, it reminded me very much of Boat Quay, Singapore.

I enjoyed several very pretty walks out to the French picquets, and old Annamese forts, in the ruins of which are tons of rice burnt to a powder. Truly, the French organ of destructiveness is very fully developed.

112

The climate of Saigon I do not think need be unhealthy if only a person takes care of himself. With a proper system of drainage and a few of the thousands of pounds which they are now wasting laid out on the improvement of the place, it might be a very pleasant residence.

It was a great treat to get some mangoes again; they do not grow in Singapore, but some of those I got in Saigon would bear comparison with the Bombay ones. They have also the Mangostin and most other tropical fruits.

Although perhaps Saigon is not the place of all others one would choose to live in, I spent a few days there pleasantly enough and am very glad that I took the trip. In addition to this, I shall be back again sooner than I could from any other place and my trip has cost me nothing.

I left in the *Granada* on the morning of the fourteenth and we are now (night of the sixteenth) well on past Pulo Aor and expect to reach Singapore, if all goes well, about six tomorrow morning.

There is a French Lieutenant on board the ship, as on board all the others, answering to an Admiralty Agent in one of our steamers. Besides him, we have only three passengers, besides myself: an old French priest and two sick doctors.

We sail under French ensign and pennant and the ships are generally reported as "H.I.M.S. So and So" and "Mons. So and So Commander", which makes our friend Haslewood, a big, jolly-looking West Countryman, very savage. He says, "The notion of taking me for a Frenchman!"

May 20th, at Singapore

Owing to a very strong contrary tide, we did not anchor in Singapore Roads till half past eight on Friday morning. We pulled down to the house and breakfasted and got into town about eleven.

Here I received your letter of April 3rd. Of the sad, sad news which it contains I cannot write much. It is so sudden and unexpected that it comes with so much greater force. Most heartily do I sympathise with poor dear Mr. and Mrs. Walpole in the great affliction which it has pleased Almighty God to send to them.

That one so young, so beautiful, should be so suddenly called away from among so many loving friends is one of those mysterious dealings of our Heavenly Father which we cannot follow. Let us hope that she is now far happier than she would have been had her life been spared, and hope that we shall meet her again in the regions of bliss when our own summons arrives. Who can tell? May not she and our darling Mary be now together, breathing a prayer over those who knew and loved them both so much on earth?

> *Not to the grave, not to the grave, my soul,*
> *Descend to contemplate*
> *The form that once was dear.*

or as Keble so beautifully has it,

> *We gladly rest*
> *Our darlings on earth's quiet breast*
> *And our hearts feel they must not break.*

The shock has been a severe one to me, more so than anyone else can or will know, and I am thankful that my absence has given me so much in the arrears of work to get through, that I have not been able to think of it so much as I otherwise should.

May 22nd

Obliged to close in a great hurry and abruptly. The *Madras* which takes the present mail fouled a ship coming down the sea and was obliged to tow her into port to prevent her foundering. No blame is to be attached to the steamer but it will give rise to a great deal of unpleasant legal business, the preliminaries of which have given us enough work to do since we came in.

June 6th

For the last four days I have been over at the office at six o'clock in the morning, working with only an hour's intermission from breakfast till after six in the evening and that, in this climate, is too much to be able to stand for long together. I am so sleepy as I begin this that I really hardly know how to put pen to paper.

With regard to borrowing money for purposes of trade, it is always a thing which I have most scrupulously avoided, though I know very well that had I been able to borrow £2,000 or £3,000 at the commencement of the China War, I might have trebled it before this. The only way in which I have felt ever justified in borrowing, as it were, is where I have seen a certain return for my money, occasionally buying things at three months' credit and selling them meanwhile for cash.[22]

It seems as if all my old friends and playmates are either getting married or else that they are being called away to a better world. So many of both have happened in the few short years that I have been out here and I often wonder within myself whether the former may be permitted to me before the latter happens. I don't think I am constituted to be an old bachelor and yet somehow I often have a kind of feeling that I shall never marry. I get low-spirited and dumpy sometimes, and then having no-one that I can talk my mind to, I fall to thinking and get indulging in curious theories which don't improve my temper and which I would never think of if I had someone to talk and argue with on the subject.[23]

Your account of poor dear Daisy's funeral is most touching and interesting. I would have given a great deal to have been there; it would have been better for me than all the sermons I ever heard in my life.

I should very much like to have one of Westmacott's casts of poor Uncle Franklin, and I should like to give you another if you would wish to have one, so if they are to be got, please order two on my account and keep one for yourself.[24]

Mr. Ritchie, I suppose, is on his way home by this time. His mission has principally been to see how expenses can be lessened in every possible way, as economy is the order of the day everywhere. Here he has ordered us to move our office in town, and discharge some of the clerks. It is true that with the office down on the wharf we shall not need so many, but it is very inconvenient indeed for the general public to have to come three miles every time they want to ask a question or perhaps ship a sample parcel. The mercantile community are up in arms about it, and it has tended more than any movement I know to make the P&O unpopular in Singapore. For us individually it is very convenient as far as our work is concerned. We are close to the house and close to the ships, but we are completely out of the world, and never know what is going on. I cannot help thinking too, that for the sake of saving £200 or £300 a year the Company will drop £2,000 or £3,000, for I do not myself believe that Singapore people will take the trouble to ship by the steamers under existing circumstances. I cannot myself help thinking that it is one of those reforms, of which there have been more than one lately, where the public convenience is not sufficiently consulted, and which, though in many points good in themselves, cannot fail to do the Company harm in the long run.

How curious that Mr. Laing should be taken so seriously ill immediately after making his first budget in Calcutta and so soon after his arrival in the country. He arrived at Penang a few days since, so ill that he could not be moved on shore, and will probably have to go home at once. Intense mental

115

fatigue and worry, I suppose, combined with the effects of climate.

It is now definitely settled that Mr. Lock is to come out and take the post of Superintendent at Hong Kong. I am very glad of it. I was sure that it would not do to part with him, and now he is settled I should not wonder if he were to bring out a wife with him. Captain Bowen is going home and has promised to call and see you if he goes near Portsmouth. I dare say you will remember him, rather a coarse old man at times, but a very good man in many ways and one who never forgets his old friends. He always speaks with great respect of poor Papa.[25]

Three of our small steamers in China have been sold at good prices, the *Chusan, Manila* and the *Rajah*. There is an immense trade springing up in the north, now that the River Yangtse is opened, and there is a good demand for steamers of all classes.

June 21st

The inconvenience of Mr. Ritchie's new system becomes more apparent now the Saigon ships come in, as they of necessity have to lie out in the Roads four miles away from us, and it is almost a day's business to get to town and back, while they are always in want of all sorts of little things, and one is obliged to go into town to attend to their requirements. However, we have no business to grumble; our business is to obey orders, but still we cannot always see things through other people's spectacles.

I do occasionally smoke a cheroot but I am not much of a smoker. Here, however, one is in the country of tobacco and the climate is a particularly relaxing one, requiring something of the sort. I do not know half a dozen people in the place who do not smoke, more or less, and assuredly the non-smokers are not the most healthy men. All the doctors recommend it, in a moderate degree, and it must be remembered that the Manila cheroots are not like the Havana cigars, as six of them are hardly equal in strength to a moderate Havana. I know many men who smoke twenty or thirty cigars a day, and twelve is considered a moderate allowance, but I very seldom exceed two and don't always take those.

There is an Admiralty Agent on board this ship, Captain Pascoe, an elder brother of your old friend, Crawford Pascoe.[26]

Poor old Johnny Borlase is the talk of the Fleet here and every naval man that one meets has some story to relate of him.[27] One of the best which is, I know, a true one, is that he was going ahead one day, under all sail and steam, when the Admiral's ship appeared ahead, crossing his bows. He immediately put his sails aback, but never stopped the engines, and the

116

consequence was that he ran full split into the Admiral, exclaiming in his broad dialect, "Oh dear, oh, dear, what shall I do? I forgot that I was a steamer!"

July 5th

I am thankful to say that I have never been better than since I have been in Singapore. The climate makes one feel a little languid sometimes, but a good game of bowls will generally set that right again. I have not required to take any medicine, even so much as a compound rhubarb pill for, I think, more than a year.

Our Directors some time ago sent out a complete diving dress to every Agency so as to have it handy in case of any emergency. The diver whom they sent out to explain the apparatus has been here for the last three weeks, and I have been down in the dress two or three times. The last time I stayed down for about a quarter of an hour, walking about the bottom. The sensation is rather novel to find oneself walking about at the bottom of the sea, but one can see all surrounding objects perfectly well, and there is no perceptible inconvenience beyond a slight sense of fullness about the ears, combined with a little headache, which goes away again almost immediately. The dress is by no means becoming and I am sure you would not know your own son in it, neither is it at all pleasant to walk about on shore, considering that the boots have leaden soles of about half a hundredweight each, and that there is a fifty-six pound weight on the chest and another on the back, besides the helmet and collar, which must weight about thirty or forty pounds. For some reason or another, a shark will never touch a man in this dress. I suppose the water bubbling up all round and the peculiar smell added to the hideous appearance of the costume frightens them.

We have been rather gay lately. Mrs. Collyer, who is an especial favourite of mine, returned a short time ago bringing her sister, Miss Dillon, with her and bringing Miss Macpherson also out. Colonel Babington, our new Brigadier, arrived about the same time in the old *Simoon* from Madras, bringing over his daughter, a lovely young girl who has just come out from England. These three young ladies are the prettiest and altogether the nicest and most unaffected girls that have been in Singapore for a long time.

We are just getting up a club here, which will be a great thing for the young unmarried men. One great advantage of it will be that it will secure admission for any of its members to the Calcutta, Bombay, Madras and Hong Kong clubs, which would be a great thing for me, in case of my being ordered away in a hurry to any of these places.

117

Do not forget my best love to the Squire when you see him. It is astonishing how among West Country people, one's name is a passport for one. I am rather a favourite at Government House simply from my being a Cornish Kendall. Both the Governor and Mrs. Cavenagh are Cornish and know a lot of Cornish relations.

August 6th

About four months ago I entered into an arrangement with some persons who ran a small steamer to and from Batavia, to supply her with coal whenever she came up, which was monthly, and I invested all my little capital in coals for her. Most suddenly and unexpectedly, her owners in Java, having had a good offer for her, have chartered her for a period of seven years, so that she is taken off the line, and what would have been a source of income of probably £100 to £120 a year has been as suddenly cut off, after being in force but a short time. I am left with a quantity of coals on hand and though, as I bought cheaply and have made a little on them, I cannot possibly lose money, yet it may be some time before I am able to realise, particularly as so few chance steamers come here now and as from our being now so far from town, one must have one's eyes pretty well open to be first in the market.

It will indeed be a loss when the fortnightly mail is taken off, but I for one do not think it at all likely that the proposed arrangement, if carried out at all, will last for more than two or three months, at the outside. The country has too heavy a stake and too deep an interest in China to lose the advantages of a regular fortnightly mail for the sake of a paltry £12,000 a year; at the same time I think the P&O Company is quite right to decline carrying the mails unless paid for it. When they, who are now paid less than half what anyone else is per mile, should be expected to run a mail at an expense of many thousands a year for nothing, I can't conceive, at the same time, it will be a terrible deprivation to us to be robbed of half our home letters.

That fire in Tooley Street seems to have been a most awful affair.[28] It is wonderful how many large fires have occurred in that neighbourhood within the past few years. I remember several myself. Mr. Braidwood's death is indeed a public calamity; he was always first on the field and so active and energetic in his measures. I have seen him several times at London fires. I can quite sympathise with poor Sheppy in her fright at the crowd, the heat and the glare at London Bridge. London Bridge Station appears to have been in considerable danger.

We have been to several very pleasant little friendly parties lately where we have generally met the three latest arrivals There seem to be about half a dozen privileged young bachelors who are generally invited out to meet them. In this category, I am happy to say that Jellicoe and I are included. It really seems to put a man on his mettle to be able to associate with clever English girls who are just out from home and who have none of the listlessness of most long residents in a hot climate.

We have lately been afflicted with a visitation of Siamese Princes and Ambassadors who have come down in a fleet of river steamers to pay a visit to the Rajah of Quedah. They are going to remain here about a week or ten days. They are a most curious-looking race of people, something between Chinese and Malay in appearance. They are indeed something like the Annamese. They appear to be very fond of finery and deck themselves out in all sorts of old uniforms so that their appearance on the Esplanade is very odd.

August 23rd

I am afraid I shall only have time to write to you one line to say that I am thankful to say that I am quite well though very busy.

We have been bothered with law business all the week, having an action pending in the Court here between the Company and the owners of an American ship, about a collision in the China Sea which occurred a little while ago.

September 7th

The *Rainbow* is just signalled from Sarawak and I believe Sir James Brooke is on board on his way to England.[29]

Our law case is not finished yet and, as the Court is adjourned for three weeks on account of the Malacca Criminal Sessions, nothing more will be done on it at present.

Our wonderful Yankee friend, Captain Johnson of the *Fire Dart*, is going home this mail having thoroughly well filled his pockets in the north of China. He means to build another steamer at once which is to "lick all creation". He says he is coming straight into New Harbour and will wake us up one fine morning with his whistle before we know he has started.

September 21st

I am not sorry that the Northerners have had a bit of a thrashing.[30] It will take down their bounce a little and I expect it will be some time before they again talk of invading Canada and attacking England.

We are having a series of photographs taken for the Directors, and I mean to make you a present of a set as soon as they are printed, so that you will get a very good idea of our buildings and neighbourhood.

October 21st

A whole month since I have written to you and three letters of yours to reply to.

Your really good and truly motherly advice about marriage is most thoroughly confirmatory of my own opinions on the subject and though one cannot tell what might happen, or what the next few years might bring forth which might change them, I do not think you need fear my being rash and headstrong in this respect. I seem to look on things in a very different light to what I did even a year or two ago and, though I trust not in a more worldly point of view, still perhaps in a more practical way. I consider myself extremely fortunate in being thrown, as I am, into the society of a number of extremely nice girls, as nice girls I am sure as one would meet anywhere in England, but still I may say that I am heart-whole at present and I see no prospect of my being in a position to allow myself to be otherwise for some to come. One cannot tell what a day may bring forth, but I hope that I may some day be able to return to old England, and I hope that when I am able to return, I may be in a position to choose a wife and that I may be able to do so.

I saw the account of a Mr. Mouilliet's delinquencies in the paper and feared it might be poor Cousin Carry's husband.[31] No doubt he is a thorough scoundrel. I wish that Caroline and her children were well quit of him. I was indeed shocked to hear of the condition that she was reduced to, but I can hardly say I was surprised.

I am happy to say that my trip to Saigon has been the means of putting about £200 into my pocket. I was lying (in the *Formosa*) alongside a very large ship which had coals on board for the French Government. The Captain wanted employment and said he intended to come to Singapore, and asked my advice about one or two things. I told him I would try and get a charter for him and two or three letters passed between us. He accordingly consigned his ship to me and when he came in, we found that the best thing he could do here would be to load here for Liverpool. Now getting a charter is simple and easy enough, but loading a ship takes time and trouble and, as particularly with our office so far from town I could not attend to his business without neglecting the Company's, I made arrangements with a merchant's house here to hand the ship over to them and share the

120

commission, so that they did all the work and I got half the pay.

Sir James Brooke goes home this time and so do Mr. and Mrs. Wilstead. We gave Sir James a ball the other day which went off very successfully. There was a good deal of speech-making at supper and we did not go home until four thirty in the morning. It was a mooted point whether it should be a public dinner or a ball, and a deputation awaited on the Rajah to ask him. He turned and asked Mrs. Wilstead which she would prefer and, of course, she said a ball. Sir James leaves his son, Captain Brooke, in charge of the Government of Sarawak, and I do not think he will ever himself come out again though he says he will if he is wanted.

We have had a great deal of trouble, bother and anxiety since last mail left in one or two matters.

In the first place the trial between the *Madras* and the *Argonaut* has been completed, and judgment is a compromise which appears to me unfair and unreasonable, and which I cannot think has not been influenced in some measure by the reputed wealth of the P&O, particularly as the Judge made use of an expression in his summing up to the effect that the loss would fall on parties who were very well able to bear it. I hope that our own people will appeal against the judgment at home, as the opinion set forth by the Judge will form a very bad precedent in the case of future trials. However, I have not time to enter into a long legal disquisition and I dare say that you would just as well be without it.

Then one of our ships, the *Formosa*, sprang a leak in harbour suddenly the other day, and the only Dock in the port was occupied at the time. She could not be kept free with the pumps and they could not work at the hole from the inside, as it was right under the condenser. At last it was determined to run her on shore, and this was done at high water and as the tide fell the engineers were able to work at the leak which they did with a will and the ship was floated next tide, and was found perfectly tight.

The latest in P&O news is that Mr. Lock is to go to Madras which I am rather surprised at, as Madras is about the smallest and least important agency in the East. I suppose however that they want to send him where he won't be able to spend much money, as he is by no means inclined to be a screw, and the Directors have got a particularly economical fit on them just now.

Our new church was opened the other day and we are now in one of the largest and handsomest churches in the East. The new organ is on its way out from England and, with that and a new organist, we shall no doubt improve the singing very much as a Quire has already been formed.

121

The latest orders of the Directors with reference to our office are that I am to make arrangements with a mercantile firm for the use of part of their office, so that I can attend town for an hour or two every day, while Jellicoe remains at New Harbour. This is a compromise which will be a great nuisance to us in dividing the office, and will not satisfy the wants of the merchants, who want a place where they can send parcels to and take delivery of them. Of course we cannot do this without a regular go-down in town and the expenses of the proposed arrangement with carriage hire, etc., are fully equal to the rent of our late regular office.

Please thank Edward for his portrait and letter. The portrait I should fancy must be a good one, but he is very much altered since I last saw him, if it is like him. He looks at least twelve or fourteen years older.

November 8th

I shall be very glad to see Mr. Terry here. He is, I believe, to sail with the new organ in the *West*. We want a good organist sadly and I have no doubt that he will meet with every co-operation and assistance from members of the congregation. How he is to exist on £200 a year though, I cannot imagine. He will doubtless though be able to get some pupils and I think it very likely that I may get him to teach me a little music.

I have heard nothing further of the Bishop coming out, but I suppose that as we are not under the Colonial Office yet, he will retain his title of Bishop of Labuan for the present.[32]

My two great favourites here, Mrs. Collyer and her sister Miss Dillon, are going home again soon, Colonel Collyer having resigned his appointment in consequence of failing health. I wish Jellicoe would make up to Miss Dillon; I am pretty sure he has only to ask. I believe he has half a mind to but is so mightily afraid of being chaffed, that he cannot make up his mind for I believe he admires her as much as I do.

There have been several daring robberies lately committed by Chinamen. The other night, a young man was woken up by feeling somebody binding his feet and, before he knew what was about, he was regularly pinioned by three Chinamen, one of whom stood over him with a knife while the other two ransacked the room, taking his watch, jewellery, sundry articles of clothing, etc., and some £50 or £60 in cash. They then thrust him into his dirty clothes' basket and shut him in by putting a big heavy box against the lid. There he remained until his servant came in at daylight in the morning.

We have sent home to the M.D.s this mail some rather curious specimens of natural history in the shape of sea worms taken from the piles of our jetties. I believe they are the largest ever seen; at least I never heard of anything approaching the size which they are. We picked three out of the head of a pile, the largest fully eighteen inches long, and the size round of a good big eel. They have a big horny head, admirably adapted for boring into wood, and they will eat into the largest pile in a very short time.

You will have heard of the accident to the Egyptian Railway by the overflowing of the Nile. This is a terrible nuisance just at the full passenger season. I expect it will not be set right for some two or three months.

November 22nd

The *Bombay*, a vessel which has just been thoroughly refitted at an expense of several thousand pounds and which is considered now a very crack ship, broke her crew shaft just outside Penang, and so was completely disabled. The mails were sent on in the small despatch steamer, which happened fortunately to be at Penang, and reached this place of course on Sunday morning.

The *Granada* also came in the same morning from Saigon, and in coming into New Harbour ran on shore about a mile from our house. We were watching her coming and saw her run on shore. Being the top of high water, she could not get off till next morning and we were in great doubts whether she was not on rocks. However, it turned out fortunately that she had found out a soft place, and as the tide went down we sent all our men down to help scrub and paint her bottom, and she floated off next morning. However, you may imagine that this was rather an anxious morning. On one side of the house seeing one of our ships going on shore, very close to a very nasty place, and on the other side watching a small steamer coming in with the P&O flag flying, from which we at once knew that something was wrong with the *Bombay*. However, things are never so bad but that they might be worse, and I was very thankful to hear that it was nothing worse than a bad breakdown.

How to get the mails on was the next question. Passengers and cargo of course remained on board the ship at Penang. The *Granada* and *Formosa* were both in port, but both under the French flag. We decided that somehow or other we must try to get one of these vessels and Jellicoe called on the new French Commander-in-Chief, who had fortunately arrived that morning in a French vessel, to ask him to let us have the *Granada*. It so happened that he had just made arrangements for going up to Saigon in the *Granada*, and he said that he should be very happy to take the mails up with him, and send them direct from Saigon. This was about the best thing that could be done

123

under the circumstances. It would be a very little loss of time going into Saigon on the way, and so we accepted the offer with pleasure. Jellicoe then offered to put coals on board for the extra voyage, but the Admiral would not hear of it, saying, "Oh, that is our charge".

So that the *Granada* still remains on her charter, and the mails go up to China entirely free of charge to the P&O. This is very good indeed of the French Admiral who I can see is a very first-rate man, and a man who knows what is what, whereas the present Commander-in-Chief is somewhat of an old lady. Frenchmen here are not accustomed to hurry themselves, and when the order was given to coal the *Granada* with all despatch, the Captain of the French man-of-war across which she was coaling stopped the coolies when it began to get dark. When this was communicated to the Admiral, he came up on deck and gave the Captain what we should call a regular wigging, before all hands. He told him that the mail service was paramount to everything else, and that he had specially given orders for the coaling to be hurried on with, that the Captain knew this and had no business to countermand his orders and so on. The Captain merely shrugged his shoulders. The state of discipline on board the French man-of-war is wonderfully lax but I expect that this Admiral will organise a very different state of things. One of the first things he intends to do is to construct a lighthouse at Cape St. James where one is badly required. His first public act has been one of great courtesy and liberality towards the English mercantile community, and he will lose nothing by it.

I am out of the way of hearing much of P&O politics in London, so that he *[Sinclair]* does not write much about what is going on. There is no doubt however that the system just now is the pruning knife, and this will I fear rid us of many of our best officers. There is much that I should like to talk to you about that I cannot well write about, but I cannot help forming an opinion on different things, and there are many matters that I should much like to see altered.

People will insist on marrying Jellicoe and he has got a number of congratulatory letters from China and elsewhere, which he doesn't half like. I hear that Macaulay is going to be married to a young lady in Melbourne with £10,000.

December 7th

I have had my hands more than usually full, and what with our having a lame duck here in the shape of the *Bombay* with a broken shaft, a ship full of stores from Hong Kong, a lot of business connected with the unfortunate

124

Malabar and other things, I really do not seem to have had ten minutes to myself since last mail left.

We shall have the *Bombay* on our hands here some little time, I expect. I am rather anxious to hear from Bombay by next mail as we shall then know definitely whether they have a shaft that can be put into her, otherwise she will have to sail back. Her opium has been landed in the store under the office, and is intensely disagreeable. The smell from it is so strong that it gives me a headache and makes one feel as drowsy as possible all day.[33]

Jellicoe has been re-elected one of the Municipal Commissioners for the present year and I have been elected Treasurer of the Masonic Lodge. This will give us both something more in the way of work to do, though neither of them is a very onerous position.

I should much like to be at home at the Great Exhibition next year if I could manage it, but at present I do not see the slightest prospect of my doing so unless Jellicoe should happen to go home and they should send someone here instead of him whom I could not get on with.

I received Harriette's portrait and am very much pleased at her kind thought of me. I am quite sure that I shall like her very much, not only because she is to be Edward's wife, but for herself, and I feel sure that she wishes to be a sister to us.

I don't know what to think of Sinclair. I sometimes think that he is not getting on as well as he might in the London office, but I don't know if he would be better off elsewhere. He has altered so much, grown up from quite a schoolboy since I saw him, that I seem to know less of him almost than Edward, although so much nearer my own age; I think perhaps a little knocking about the world would not do him any harm and might be of great service to him, but if he comes out here in the P&O service, he must be prepared to learn and work and not to mind a few discouragements and vexations.

I am very thankful to be in a place like Singapore, and I trust that I may not be removed elsewhere, at any rate in any other position than Agent. Society is so free from cliqueism here, and there are so few P&Os of a low stamp known to people in the place, that I take a far better position than I should probably be able to elsewhere. I am not, as a rule, fond of exclusively P&O society, and one must get a good deal of it in a place like Bombay.

January 9th, 1862

We have had another lame duck here, the *Emeu* arriving of course on Sunday, and taking all our resources and energies to get her ready to go on to China. We got rid of her at seven this morning, and the *Pekin* with the other mail goes at ten!! Fancy despatching two mail steamers within three hours and with only two hands to depend on for everything. *Pekin* crammed full with passengers, and *Emeu* with a lot of cargo.

Misfortunes never come singly. After getting over the *Bombay's* mishap so beautifully, here comes the *Emeu* in broken down, and we hear from Hong Kong that the *Columbian* is missing, out fourteen days from hence, while the average passage at this time of year is only eight or nine.

You will know of the melancholy news which poor Jellicoe received last mail. He will undoubtedly have, I think, to go home in the course of a mail or two and assist his poor mother in these property disputes. I am rather anxious to know whether the Managing Directors will give me charge of the Agency during his absence. I hope they will and cannot help thinking that I should do better for them than anyone else, at any rate as Acting Agent, as I am well acquainted with everyone in Singapore and with the peculiar ways and habits of the place. One thing I will tell you *entre nous*, that if they do not let me take it, you will probably see me in England, but of course everything must depend on circumstances.

January 21st

Before I go on to anything else, I must speak of the heavy tidings which your last letter has brought of Harriette. With you, I cannot understand it, but I fully and deeply sympathise with poor Edward in his great trial. I do hope that it may yet be alright. I can never believe that it is her own doing, for from all that I know and have heard of her, she is the last person in the world whom I should believe to be capable of such an act.

Jellicoe has been very seedy and will, I think, certainly go home by the mail after next, if not next mail, leaving me in charge of the Agency. I only hope that the M.D.'s will allow me to retain it during his absence, and I am the more induced to believe such a thing possible as I am thoroughly well acquainted with the place and the customs and habits of its people, both European and native. I think Jellicoe is a good deal cut up by his poor father's death, and there is likely to be some dispute with the Baronet about the property, so that his presence is absolutely essential at home. The immediate cause of his going is however a sick certificate which the Doctor has given him without knowing anything of his family matters or of his wishing to go home on private business.

We had telegraphic news by last mail of the death of the Prince Consort and all flags have been half-mast ever since.[34] We have received no particulars yet but shall probably hear by next mail. What a blow it will be for our poor little Queen. I should not at all wonder if it has a most serious effect on her mind.

I hope we have done with breakdowns for the present; we have had enough of them lately, but misfortunes never come singly. We have a ship here now in dock, and are likely to have some trouble with her officers which is a great source of anxiety and worry. Baynton is dismissed the service by orders from home, a great pity, for it was nothing that could be attributed to his fault: some informality in getting coal receipts which he appears to have had very little to do with. I am very sorry for him for he is one of the best officers down there, and there are others who could have been spared.

February 7th

The news of the Prince Consort's death reported last mail by telegraph is fully confirmed this time. There will not be a person in the world who has heard or knows anything of our poor dear little Queen who will not sincerely sympathise with her. It seems more as if someone belonging to one's own family had been called away than a person whom one absolutely knew nothing of here, except by reputation, but our little Queen had so bound herself up in the affections of her people that any blow happening to her cannot but be felt as a national one. She appears to bear her loss as she does everything else, with true Christian fortitude, and let us hope that strength may not be denied to her, which will alone enable her to bear her sorrow with resignation. I much feared that the terrible event coming with such sudden force upon her might have been too much for her.

Jellicoe is going by next mail and we are, as you may imagine, busy enough in getting ready for his departure. Young Barnes has come down from Hong Kong to join the office and with his assistance I shall be perfectly able to carry on the work of the Agency till Jellicoe's return.

The Bishop of Calcutta was here the other day and consecrated our new church. He preached an excellent and thoroughly practical sermon on the occasion and it was a great treat to hear him, as our own Padre is not the most eloquent.

The Collyers are going home by next mail I am sorry to say, and, sad to relate, Miss Dillon goes home as Miss Dillon, and unless Jellicoe should do something to prevent it she will last as such in England, I think. Colonel Collyer growls at going home with £1,300 a year to retire upon. I think he will try for some appointment at home, probably Superintendent of Convict

127

Prisons, the same as Colonel or Captain, I forget which, Gambier, which I believe he has been offered.

The Town Hall was to have been opened on sixth February, the grand day in Singapore being the anniversary of the foundation of the Settlement, with a Grand Ball but, in consequence of the general mourning, it has been postponed. I am afraid that most, if not all, of the young ladies will have gone before we have it.

The old Tumongong died the other day, and is succeeded by his eldest son, Prince Inchee Wan Aboobakar, of whom you have often heard me speak. We were invited to the funeral, which was a curious sight. The body was placed in a coffin covered with Cashmere shawls, and was put on a large platform which was born on the shoulders of a large number of men. On this platform round the body were a number of attendants, some of them carrying huge yellow and white umbrellas, and others scattering small coins and handfuls of rice coloured with saffron among the crowd as they passed. There was a general scramble for the rice and I had one of the coins given to me, and mean to put it on my watch chain as a memento. The platform was carried up the hill to the grave and placed over the grave; the coffin was then lowered down, and there was a general scramble for the cloth, with which the platform was covered, which was torn into thousands of pieces, and each Malay who could get a piece possessed himself of one. When the coffin reached the bottom of the grave, which was about nine feet deep, a priest and another man got down and opened the coffin, chanting a low monotonous kind of prayer; while this was going on the grave was covered up with shawls, but those who were near could look under the shawls and see that the body was swathed tightly and embedded in a large quantity of rice, I conclude as provisions for it during the journey. The grave was then closed up. The general rush and apparent indifference manifested by the Malays, although the old man was very much respected among them, contrasted very forcibly with our simple and affecting burial service, and one could not help thinking of the difference between the Christian and Mahomedan faith, and wishing that one could see these numbers of intelligent men brought to a knowledge of the truth.

February 19th

You may imagine that I shall be very sorry indeed to lose Jellicoe; no two men could get on together better than we have done in every way and I think we have been a mutual assistance to each other. I have much, very much, to thank him for; no-one could have been kinder or more like a brother to me than he has been, but I hope and believe that he will not be away for long. I am left in charge of the Agency; whether the Directors will permit me to retain it or not, I cannot of course say.

Brother Jonathan may bluster, but there are many men of sound common sense among his leading men; the only fear is that mobocracy may be too strong for the opinions of a few.[35] I think that most of the Americans out here, at any rate the best of them that I know, have condemned the seizure of the Commissioners as a most unwise and injudicious proceeding, though there is no doubt that there is an opinion that it was a smart thing to do.

There is to be a Grand Ball tonight to celebrate the opening of the Town Hall. It was to have been held on the sixth but, everyone being in mourning, it was decided that it had better be put off. Now so many young ladies are going away, it could not be put off any longer.[36]

March 6th

I shall be rather in a state of suspense for the next few mails to know what the M.D.'s intend to do, as they write by this last mail in anticipation of Jellicoe going home, to say that they have appointed Macaulay to the Agency and have sent out orders to him to come up here. Now Macaulay is down in Sydney and cannot be up here for some time. Whether, when they find that Jellicoe only wants to be at home for a short time, they will countermand the order or not, I cannot tell. It appears certain that they have got hold of the idea, which is generally prevalent out here, that Jellicoe has come in for a large fortune and wants to resign the service altogether, whereas, poor fellow, he is not going home on the pleasantest business and does not want to be at home longer than he can help.

The Managing Directors have again rather gone out of their way to be civil to us for the way in which we managed the despatch of the *Bombay's* mails and the repairs and re-despatch of the ship, and I think and hope that these little things will tell up in Jellicoe's favour.

Sutherland passed on by the mail.[37] He went home rather under a cloud, I think, but has come out with every full authority, and is to be Superintendent at Hong Kong. We have few men with better heads and more enlightened and refined ideas than Sutherland has. He has mixed more in society than Macaulay has and is a thorough man of business without being too Scotch. He was telling me that if I could see my way at all he would recommend me to take a run home in a year or so, at any rate. He thinks that a man ought to go home once every five years and I agree with his theory. He gives himself a rubbing up, physically and mentally, and at the same

129

time lets the powers that be know that he is alive, whereas it is occasionally with them, out of sight, out of mind, at any rate to some extent.

We had a very pleasant regimental party, a farewell to the Babingtons, a few days ago. The sepoys took their horses out and dragged the carriage up the hill by torch light, a very pretty sight. You will perhaps think it is as well for me that they are going away, inasmuch as I might be falling in love with one of the young ladies, a very possible contingency I must admit as, search all England through, you will hardly find two nicer girls or a nicer father and mother. However, they are going and I don't think it is likely that I shall see them again. Such is life!

I shall be very glad to get poor Uncle Franklin's medallion as soon as I can get an account from Sinclair. I will send home more money to pay for it if there is not sufficient at home.

March 21st

Our Bishop has been out here for some time and I have seen a good deal of him, though not very much of his wife. I called one day and she was out, and I was only introduced to her today for the first time. They both remember you and the Bishop thinks he remembers Mary at Portsmouth, but does not remember her at Calcutta except by name.

Lots of our officers are leaving the service in China, and one can hardly wonder at it. Many of the best men have gone, lured by the tempting salaries offered from so many new ports opening up. There is lots of money to be made up there now, but in my opinion things are going ahead too fast to last. The place will soon be flooded with steamers, and I believe that in a year or so we shall hear of a grand smash, when things will resume a more natural and healthy footing; meanwhile large fortunes will be made by enterprising men.

We have had a terrific mortality among our dogs the last three days, having lost five and all the others being sick. I don't know what can be the matter with them, whether they have been poisoned or not, but we are left now with very little outside protection and I have, therefore, loaded my revolver in case of anyone wishing to pay us a visit at night.

Economy is the order of the day with the French out here now. They are sending ships and troops home from Saigon almost every day and I expect that they will very soon give up our vessels. I believe the new French Commander has worked a great change in Saigon and it is about time he did for I never in my life saw such waste of money as is going on there, or rather was when I was there.

April 8th

I got the medallion of poor Uncle Franklin and am very pleased with it. Though I can hardly remember him, yet I can trace a likeness and I believe that all those who knew him will think that it is very good indeed.

May 4th

First of all, I must tell you that Macaulay has arrived and has taken charge of the Agency. I think you know exactly what my opinion of Macaulay is. Out of the office, I like him as a rule very much but he is so crotchety and eccentric that he is by no means a pleasant man to work with. It is not altogether comfortable for a man to have to give up the head of his table to a complete stranger in the place, but when that person immediately he gets there orders about his servants as if they were dogs, and seems to consider everything in the place to belong to himself, it is doubly unpleasant. I do not think that he will be liked in Singapore because, in the first place, he has set his face against conforming to any of the usages of the place. He says he shall not call on anyone and therefore he will know nobody. I hope for his own sake that he will modify his views on this subject; if not, the P&O Agent I am sure will not be the popular man that he has always been there. Already I am being continually told by the principal merchants in the place that they are very sorry that I am ousted and that they hope that as I am not to remain, Jellicoe will soon be out again.

I think that as Barnes is likely to remain here, it will be a good opportunity for me to try to get a run home. I shall wait till I hear of Jellicoe's arrival in England, and his reception there, and then I think it is not unlikely that the next steamer may take home an official application from me for six months' leave of absence. Indeed, I am sure that I must have a thorough change soon if I am to keep my health, though I am not now by any means ill, but I don't want to have to wait until I must get a sick certificate for going home, and I think I have been out here long enough now to entitle me to a spell.

You may conceive that I was horrorstruck at the news which your last letter brought about poor dear Pelyn being burnt. Most heartily do I sympathise with its dear good owner in this new affliction which has come upon him. I hope that the damages, pecuniarily, may not fall so heavily as is at first anticipated, for there are few persons who can so ill afford to be burnt out. The destruction of the wine cellar is no doubt a source of very great mortification, though of course that is nothing to the fact of the poor old house having gone. The poor Squire, I do indeed pity him from the bottom of my heart. Verily, he seems born to trouble but, as you say, it is no doubt for some good end that such is permitted.

You will be glad to hear that I have had Lady Franklin here. She came down in the *Fiery Cross*. Both she and Miss Cracroft are looking very well and are, I think, enjoying their travel very much. She very kindly gave me a copy of McClintock and another book, which I don't suppose will be much use to me, "Notes on Nursing" by Florence Nightingale, but any book presented by Lady Franklin is of value. I shewed them as well as I could all over the place and asked one or two gentleman friends to meet them in the evening at dinner. They will be going on by the mail which takes this, and will I hope be able to give you a good report of me on their arrival in England. Curiously enough, the medallion which I have of poor Uncle Franklin was the first which my aunt had seen, and although I do not think she was altogether satisfied with it, she was pleased to see it in this part of the world.

May 20th

I have not been fit for much the last fortnight as I have been bothered with a nasty bilious attack, and if I don't soon get over it, I may have to seek a change. It is the most trying time of year just now and everyone seems to have been more or less laid up. I am sure that I must soon have a thorough change of air if I am to keep my health and yet I don't want to be sent home on sick certificate if I can help it. I have asked the Directors for six months' leave which I have every hope they will give me, and then I hope, after a run home, I shall be able to take up my old duties again like a giant refreshed.

Things are jogging along as usual but it is easy to see that Macaulay will not suit Singapore and I think everybody will be looking forward to Jellicoe's return, though I flatter myself that if I had remained here in charge, people would not have been so displeased. Indeed, I have received the most flattering expressions of sympathy in my being superseded from many of the principal men in Singapore.

Mr. Lock has got the Stamps Office in Madras, a bit of jobbery everyone says, but a very good thing for him. It is an appointment worth some £2,500 or £3,000 a year. He has married a Miss Pennycuick, sister I believe of my old schoolfellow. The Madras Agency will now be vacant and one of the few able men whom the P&O have out in the East will be lost to them.

We had a little excitement the other day with the *Salsette*. She broke adrift during the night, and after playing all sorts of mad antics, finally deposited herself high and dry at the bottom of our garden. Fortunately she was undamaged and floated with the tide, but it might have been a very serious matter.

May 30th
I have only time for one line, to tell you that I have been rather seedy and that, after consulting with the Doctor, I have decided on taking a run on to China. The sea voyage I hope will set me up completely, and I shall then be able to say that I have been to China, before I go home.

I hope that I might be able to get leave to go home so as to be able to start in September, and should that be the case, I daresay Sinclair would like to put off his holiday until my arrival so that we may be able to take a walking tour through the Midland counties or a run on the Continent together. Sinclair will, of course, be able to find out whether and when they will allow me to go and you will know therefore when to expect me. I should very much like to get home before the closing of the Exhibition, but fear that it will not be possible.

June 6th, at Hong Kong
On board ship, and especially an opium ship, is not the place to write, and I am sorry to say that I have put off beginning a letter to you till my arrival here.[38] Since I came here, I have had so much to see and so many little things to do, that I have now only a few minutes left before starting for Shanghai to say that I have got so far on my journey safely and pleasantly and am thankful to say that my trip has done me a great deal of good.

If I can find a steamer going over to Japan from Shanghai, I shall certainly run over to Nagasaki, but I fear it is unlikely or at any rate uncertain.

I am afraid that I just shan't get leave in time to go home for the Great Exhibition; I either just shall or just shan't. It would be very tantalising just to miss it but, anyhow, I hope that I may spend Christmas with you if all goes well.[39]

June 12th, at Shanghai
One line to say that I am here all safely, after a very pleasant voyage, and have just made arrangements to start for Nagasaki this afternoon.[40]

August 20th, at Singapore
I heard from Jellicoe by post that it was alright and that my leave was granted. If so, I shall hear about it in all probability by next mail, and you may expect to see me in about a fortnight after the receipt of this letter! I

can hardly realise the fact that another fortnight will most likely see me on my way to the dear old country, but I hope it may. I shall of course go through France, and may possibly telegraph my arrival if I find it worthwhile, so do not be surprised or frightened if you should happen to get a telegram.

All the furniture, etc., in the house is to be sold on Friday. We have cleared out. I am living at the Club, Macaulay at the Hotel and Barnes is at present staying with a friend till other arrangements are decided on. I have been working like a coolie the last day or two, packing, sorting, numbering, etc., etc., etc., and shall be very glad when it is all over and things are a little settled. Macaulay will not go to the expense of furniture, etc., but I think it not unlikely that he may buy up sufficient to furnish a bedroom and a small dining table, etc., and come to live at the house again. He will find it very uncomfortable at the Hotel.

You will have heard from Sinclair all about my leave and so will know whether and when to expect me.

The warm and cordial welcome which I have received from all my friends on my return here would render me unwilling to quit again for any place but old England. People were kind enough to drown me in a typhoon and more than one person lifted up their hands in astonishment at seeing me, and two or three had that very day written to friends in England and elsewhere to tell of my melancholy fate. I succeeded in getting P.S.'s put to two letters to say that I had arrived safe and sound.

Mrs. Cavenagh and the Governor have been very kind and welcomed me back quite like old friends. Within a few hours after it was known that I had come back, I received an invitation card to dinner at Government House, and I am engaged somewhere nearly every evening till my departure.[41]

NOTES

1. Edward was Kendall's clergyman brother, on his way to Toronto, but who later returned to settle in Britain.

2. Brunel's *Great Eastern* made her first voyage to New York in 1860 and came near to disaster when, in a storm, she lost most of her sails and smashed her paddles.

3. Flags or semaphore signals were hoisted at many ports to announce the arrival of the mail ships. In some ports, such as Aden, a signal gun was fired.

4. See entry for January 21st, 1861.

5. I can find no record of an explosion in the *Great Western*. There was, however, an explosion in the funnel casing of the *Great Eastern* at around this time.

6. The explorer, Sir John Franklin, sailed on a new expedition to find the North West Passage in May 1845 in *Erebus* and *Terror*. The ships were last seen in June 1845 and it was another fourteen years before the mystery of their disappearance was discovered. Three

search expeditions failed to find the lost one and in 1857, after Eskimos were found to be in possession of articles belonging to members of the lost expedition, Lady Franklin organised her own search by Captain Francis (later, Sir Francis) McClintock. In 1859, McClintock, who had sailed on the previous searches, was able to reveal the fate of Franklin's expedition: Franklin having died on June 11th, 1847 after having discovered the Passage. Lady Franklin died in 1875, aged 83.

7. Captain Robert McLure served on two of the Franklin search expeditions. On the latter, he completed the work connected with the discovery of the North West Passage and was rewarded by a knighthood.

8. The Revd Francis McDougall was Bishop of Labuan between 1854 and 1868. While in the East, he translated the Book of Common Prayer into Malay.

9. Kendall's comments refer to Samuel Laing who was Finance Minister in India in 1860. The suppression of the Mutiny had increased the debt of India and, to correct the deficiency, customs duties were reorganised and income tax and licence duties imposed. See also his entry on June 6th, 1861.

10. Owned by the Eagle Line, *Royal Charter* left Australia for Liverpool with a cargo of gold, 390 passengers returning home from the Australian Gold Rush, and 112 crew. In October 1859 she was blown onto the rocks in Anglesey by a freak hurricane which sank many ships and killed about 800 people. Although *Royal Charter* was wrecked within walking distance of dry land, the huge waves battered to death most of the passengers. The wrecking achieved notoriety due to the amount of looting and by the fact that, although the ship was so close to shore, so many lives were lost.

11. There is here a gap of one year in Kendall's letters.

12. The missing policeman turned out to have been hiding in the jungle and appeared the following day. Around fourteen people were arrested following this riot.

13. In December 1860, the Royal Mint abandoned copper coinage in favour of the more durable bronze. Much interest was aroused by the change to bronze, the reduction in size of the penny, halfpenny and farthing and by the use of a new portrait of the Queen.

14. By this time, passengers were able to shorten their journey times by travelling overland by rail and joining their ship at Marseilles. The French insistence on passengers having passports and visas was an irritant as passengers considered themselves as being in transit through France. The Emperor was Napoleon III, nephew of Bonaparte.

15. A European interpreter, Mr Richardson, was murdered outside the gates of the British Legation. A number of murders followed, including that of Heusken the popular secretary to the American Legation in January 1861. Kendall was right in his forecast; on 24 March, Japanese extremists assassinated the hated Regent as he was proceeding in state to the Shogun's castle in Yedo.

16. Following his inauguration at Washington on March 4th, Lincoln was faced with the problem that, while seven slave states had seceded, eight still remained in the Union. At this stage, Lincoln was desperately trying to keep the peace.

17. The accident occurred at Epsom Junction on 28 January, 1861, when the express train to Portsmouth jumped the rails and some of the carriages ran down an embankment. One passenger was killed and nineteen injured. Kendall's own railway accident experience occurred at Lewisham Old Station on June 28th, 1857, when a train ran into the back of a stationary train. Twelve people were killed and sixty-two injured.

18. Middle Java was struck in 1861 by flooding of three major rivers in which a great number of people lost their lives and considerable damage was sustained. In the Netherlands, extensive flooding was caused because of drift-ice on the rivers Rhine and Waal.

19. Dr. Temple, a distinguished social reformer who became Archbishop of Canterbury

in 1897, was Headmaster of Rugby at this time. He contributed in 1860 to the Essays and Reviews and while his contribution was unexceptional, it became associated with the extreme views of other contributors. The Guardian mentioned by Kendall was an Anglican newspaper of the day.

20. A Major in the Royal Artillery and the eldest son of Viscount Avonmore, William Yelverton married Miss Longworth in an invalid form of ceremony in April 1857. Over a year later, he formally married a widow, Mrs. Forbes. Miss Longworth claimed to be Yelverton's wife and unsuccessfully sued him for restitution of conjugal rights. The matter was unsuccessfully raised in the Irish and Scottish Courts and, finally, in the House of Lords in 1867.

21. The Spanish Government sent 850 Tagal troops from the Philippines to Saigon in 1857 to assist the French colonialists in the conquest of the cities of Tourane and Saigon. The Tagals who stayed behind afterwards were assigned to the French Army.

22. See Kendall's entry for August 6th, 1861.

23. Kendall was married on 30 April, 1867 in Australia to Miss Frances Fletcher. She was the daughter of the Revd. William Fletcher (then Senior Chaplain in Bombay) and his wife Elizabeth.

24. There is no trace of a bust of Franklin having been executed by any Westmacott.

25. Edward Kendall died in 1845. While Superintendent at Southampton, he proposed that the Company extended its services to Australia, a plan eventually achieved in 1852 on the prompting of Pascoe. It is possible that Pascoe, being a close friend of the Kendall family, took up the idea of an extension to Australia when Edward died. Edward Kendall had served on several Arctic expeditions and Cape Kendall on Southampton Island in the Arctic Circle was named after him. Edward was a popular man in Southampton and, at his death, all flags in the town and in the harbour were flown at half mast and all the shops closed on the day of his funeral.

26. At a club in Hong Kong in 1846 Lt. Crawford Pascoe R.N. suggested that P&O run a branch line from Singapore to Australian ports. Among the group was the editor of the local newspaper who asked him to write an article. Pascoe did so and the article had a marked effect on the P&O plans. He was on board *Chusan* on her historic voyage to Australia.

27. Captain John Borlase was commanding the *Pearl*, a screw steamer corvette, on the East Indies and China station. He had been appointed to her on 23rd August, 1859 and, after almost two years, one would have thought that he would have become accustomed to the ship! The incident did his career no harm for he retired as a Vice-Admiral.

28. The Tooley Street fire occurred on Sunday, 22nd June, 1861 and was considered one of the largest fires that London had experienced since the Great Fire of 1666. It started in Cotton's Wharf and spread to Hay's and Chamberlain's Wharves and to St. Olav's Church, threatening London Bridge Station at one time. The fire burned all week and erupted again on Thursday when molten wax which had collected in the network of vaults beneath the warehouses burst into flame. A direct result of the fire, which was finally extinguished on 18 July, was the establishment of the Metropolitan Fire Brigade which took over the fire services which had previously been operated by the Insurance companies for whom Mr Braidwood acted as chief fire-fighter.

29. Sir James Brooke was the hereditary Sultan of Sarawak which had been in the Brooke family since 1841. *Rainbow* was Brooke's own yacht.

30. The first major battle of the American Civil War took place at Bull Run on 21st July, 1861. Here, the determined defence of "Stonewall" Jackson halted the Northern Union troops who were then driven back behind the Washington defences. The battle shook the North into realising that the war would require their maximum efforts.

136

31. The Times of 17 July, 1861 reported that Louis Moulliet was charged with fraud following his obtaining a loan on the security of some casks of wine which were afterwards found to contain water.

32. In August 1858, the Government of India passed from the Honourable East India Company to the Colonial Office. Clearly it was taking time for all the various functions to be completely handed over to the various Crown offices.

33. Although Britain had largely ceased the importation of opium into China at this time, it was still being imported, against the wishes of the Chinese Government, by foreign traders.

34. Prince Albert became ill in November with what appeared to be influenza, but which proved to be typhoid fever, and he died on December 14th. Kendall was right, the Queen was profoundly affected by Albert's death.

35. "We must consult Brother Jonathan" is said to have been a frequent remark of George Washington's, referring to Jonathan Trumbull, Governor of Connecticut. The incident referred to is the "Trent Affair". In 1862, President Jefferson appointed two Commissioners to go to France and England to sell cotton and to negotiate for the recognition of the Confederacy. *Trent* (a neutral ship) was stopped on the high seas by an American warship and the two Commissioners were taken prisoner and taken to Boston. The incident created a diplomatic row which was quickly forgotten when Lincoln ordered the release of the two men.

36. Young ladies going out East looking for husbands with prospects were known as the "Fishing Fleet". Those returning home unsuccessful were unkindly referred to as the "Returned Empties".

37. Thomas Sutherland had a distinguished career with P&O and, like Kendall, started overseas life in Bombay. He was appointed Managing Director of P&O in 1872 and in 1880, at the age of 46, was appointed Chairman, a position which he held until his death 34 years later. He was awarded the G.C.M.G. and was for some time an M.P. While Superintendent at Hong Kong, he founded the Hong Kong and Shanghai Bank.

38. It is likely that Kendall travelled in this instance by one of the French steamers.

39. The second Great Exhibition which was held in London in 1862 was marred by the death of Prince Albert who had been closely involved in its planning. It is likely that Kendall did get home in time for Christmas.

40. It is not known how Kendall got to Nagasaki and, unfortunately, we have no description of his visit there or to Hong Kong and Shanghai.

41. At this point, Kendall returned home to the UK on leave.

6 The Confederate sloop of war *Alabama*, 1863.

7
On Board "Vectis", "Orissa" and "Columbian"

September 16th, 1863, at Grand Hotel, Paris

We were in ample time at London Bridge, and took our tickets through to Marseilles, with the option of staying up to fifteen days at any place en route.

At Folkestone we found a very fine and fast steamer, the *Victoria*, which brought us over to Boulogne in an hour and a quarter. The weather was most delightful, sufficient breeze to make it beautifully cool and pleasant and to give the people forward an occasional ducking with spray, but very little sea on and consequently few people sick. Sinclair is naturally crowing a good deal at not being sick on the way over and it is something to say as some people were and others, particularly ladies, imbibed sufficient bottle porter and brandy to make them so.

We took a bit of a walk about Boulogne before starting, saw some soldiers drilling and had a good look at rather a fine church in the Place Imperiale.

The train was off about four and we had a very pleasant though rather tedious journey up. There are immense numbers of English about everywhere, in fact, one seems to meet more English than French, almost. We came up in the carriage with an old lady and gentleman, who are bound for Marseilles, but I did not find out whether we were to be fellow passengers. His nationality was unmistakable from his jolly red face and white hair, and from his constantly wanting to know what was the French for 76.

We reached Paris in good time, and drove to this place which is the most luxurious and handsomely-fitted place of the kind that I ever saw, exceeding even the Louvre. We have most splendid apartments, and not much fear of not being tired enough to go to sleep when one gets into bed, as there are about 150 stairs to mount to it. We have not yet fixed our plans for today and tomorrow, except that we start tomorrow evening at 7.45 p.m. for Lyons, spending Friday in Lyons and getting to Marseilles on Saturday morning. The steamer leaves at seven am on Sunday.

I wonder how long it will be before I see the white cliffs of Dover again. I feel rather like a little boy going back to school again.

September 19th, at Marseilles

I only wish that we had been able to spend a month in Paris instead of a

139

couple of days but as it was we managed I think to see as much as possible of Paris in the time. We are now tolerably tired, Sinclair particularly so as he cannot manage to sleep in a railway carriage as well as I do.

On Wednesday, we drove all round the Boulevards and principal streets of Paris, saw the Champs-Elysées, the Arc de Triomphe, Champs de Mars, Ecole Militaire, etc., and went all over the Palace of the Luxembourg and the Hotel de Cluny. We also went over the Panthéon or Church of Sainte Geneviève, Notre Dame and the Madeleine.

We had a most magnificent dinner at the Table d'Hôte of the Grand Hotel to which some three or four hundred sat down.

In the evening took a stroll through most of the principal streets and visited a café chantant or "singing coffee" as Tomkins calls it, and the Château des Fleurs, which is a large garden laid out something in the style of Cremorne, where there was some very fair music and a little dancing which we watched for a while but found rather slow, so we went on with our walk along the whole length of the Champs-Elysées and Rue de Rivoli up the Boulevard de Sebastopol and along the other Boulevard home. A tolerably long walk and we were not sorry, I assure you, to get to bed.

Next morning after breakfast, we started and walked to Pere-Lachaise. There was a very pretty funeral procession going into the cemetery as we got there; a little girl followed to the grave by some dozen or so of her playmates all dressed in white. We waited and saw the whole of the ceremony and after walking through the cemetery, which is very pretty but which I was a little disappointed in, we took a carriage and returned by another route.

I don't think that I admire Pere-Lachaise as much even as Kensal Green, though the different characteristics of the two nations are interesting. There are, I think, more really pretty monuments in Kensal Green, though there are few really ugly ones in Pere-Lachaise, but there is an air of trumpery about many of the monuments in the latter that there is not so much of in the former.[1]

In the afternoon, we strolled about a little, saw the Louvre and the Tuileries and went into the garden of the Tuileries but did not see the Musée du Louvre as it required a stamped ticket for admission, and we had no spare time for that.

We dined at a restaurant and started for the 7.45 express train at Lyons. Although we had our baggage booked and were ready at least six minutes before the time, they wouldn't let us go by that train, but as there was another express leaving at eight, we caught that. It was rather tantalising though to see the other train start while we were locked in, but French railway officials are very arbitrary.

We got to Lyons about seven yesterday morning, and after breakfast at the Buffet drove to one of the hotels where we had a bath and then drove all round the city. It is a handsome town with some very fine streets and a few large public buildings. There is a beautiful public park, about two miles out, which we visited and were much charmed with the scenery on the banks of the Sâone and Rhône. We had some oysters and lemon with a bottle of chablis for tiffin, and very good both eatables and drinkables they were, though we went to a little pokey place in a back street for them.

We started by the 10.45 p.m. train, travelling all night again, and arriving here (Marseilles) about seven a.m. today. After a bath at the hotel we turned regularly into bed, and got up to breakfast at eleven afterwards, drove round the place and went on board the *Vectis*, returning soon, so as to have a good nap before dinner.

September 25th, on board *Vectis*

The day we left Malta was, I think, without exception the most uncomfortable day I ever spent on board ship. A nasty rolling swell that made the vessel tumble and jump about in every direction and a hot sirocco wind which was, if you can imagine such a thing, damp and muggy and yet parching. No-one was up to anything and most people spent the greater part of the day in bed. I did for one, not from actual sea sickness, but from there being no sense of comfort elsewhere. I got up to dinner, at which as you may imagine there was a very poor attendance.

We have a pleasant enough lot of fellow passengers, who seem all to have settled down at once to their sea life, without grumbling and fault-finding. There are only three ladies on board, but I expect we shall pick up several from the Southampton steamer.

I don't altogether like going to Hong Kong instead of Singapore as it seems rather throwing away what one has hitherto done towards making a standing and position for oneself, and although I don't go out quite as a stranger to the place, I have no interests there, and but few friends, whereas I know that I may speak with confidence in saying that I should be publicly welcomed in Singapore. I am somebody there, nobody in Hong Kong, and human nature cannot help feeling satisfaction in knowing that one is respected and appreciated. However, I trust it is all for the best, and I hope that I may sometime or other be permitted to take the reins of office at Singapore again. Sutherland will have, when I get there, three men who

141

have been P&O Agents serving under him, Capt. Caldbeck, Dalziel and myself. I expect there will very probably be some changes 'ere long and I hope that any move may tend to see me upwards.

September 26th

Rather rougher and hotter, but all going on well, and expecting to anchor in Alexandria about one o'clock. I don't know whether at present Sinclair will be able or not to go any way across the desert with me. If the Mauritius mail is not up he may be able to do so, and I hope he will for his own sake.

October 1st, on board *Orissa*

I last wrote to you just before I left the *Vectis* and we expect to reach Aden the day after tomorrow.

We have just passed the *Candia* with the homeward Calcutta mail, but not near enough to communicate with her except by signal, so that we could not write to her, but I hope that we may just catch the homeward Bombay mail at Aden.

Poor old Sinclair saw but little of Egypt as he was only just able to come on shore with me as far as the train, and then go back again at once as the *Vectis* only stayed about four hours in port. I should much like him to have seen something more of Egypt, but it was hardly worthwhile for him to wait by himself and I knew nobody in Cairo to recommend him to.

It was just a question of whether we should be able to go on in the railway the whole way to Cairo, as the Nile has risen so rapidly and so high this season that they were afraid of the railway sinking. However, we went slowly over the flooded parts and managed to get on without having to exchange the railway carriage for the horrors of the Nile boat. We got to Cairo about midnight and they made us turn out and go to the hotel to sleep, though we had started with the idea of going straight through to Suez. This was rather a sell, for though we were none of us sorry to get a comfortable bed to sleep in and a good bath in the morning, we had to travel the whole way across the desert in the heat of the sun, instead of by night, and had some 14/- or 15/- a head to pay as the generality of people had. I never pay anything travelling overland as the Company pay hotel bills.

I think Sinclair was struck with the picturesqueness, filth and laziness of the Arabs and you certainly do begin to feel the getting Eastward when you get as far as Egypt. In every little thing, you notice the effect of laziness and want of finish. Even the railway carriages, which have originally been handsome first-class carriages, are dirty and full of dust, their brasswork has never been touched since they came out and the nettings are all broken. Everything, in fact, is slovenly and there seems a lack of energy in everything and everybody. It is a pity we cannot get the management of the railway into our own hands; we would have things a little different, I expect.

After a pleasant enough journey across the desert, considering the dust, which is what you have no possible conception of in England, we got to Suez about one p.m. on Sunday, and after a good wash and a good dinner at the hotel, found our way on board the *Orissa* and started away about seven.

It is desperately hot, but we have plenty of ice and punkahs going and so we can bear it. We are very luxurious, having ice creams for tiffin and other acceptable blessings not always to be met with on board ship, and lots of room. I have two good cabins, and may have another if I like. We are about forty First-Class passengers and everyone has a cabin to himself, with plenty to spare.

We have morning service every day at ten o'clock, a practice which is not generally observed but which Parrish always has on board his ship, and there is a very full attendance of passengers every day, much more so than I have ever seen before.[2]

We heard at Suez just as we were starting of the breakdown of the *Poonah* with the outward mails of the 20th. I am afraid that this may make the Calcutta mail late, and so delay me in Ceylon so that I shall not be able to stay as long as I hoped to do in Singapore.

October 3rd

We are expecting to reach Aden this afternoon, soon after dinner.

We have been busy all the last two days practising for Sunday. Parrish has a very fair harmonium on board which Mrs. Hempsted has consented to play and my "Hymns, Ancient and Modern", the only copy on board the ship, have been in great requisition. We have arranged chants for the Venite and Jubilate in the morning and for the Magnificat and Nunc Dimittis in the evening and the following hymns: Morning: Advent Hymn and My God, My Father. Evening: Old Hundredth and Sun of My Soul.

October 13th, at Adelphi Hotel, Bombay

Here I am again in this delectable place which, bad as it always was, has not much improved, I think, since my time here. It is, however, a relief to be on shore again anywhere, for though the *Orissa* is the most comfortable vessel I know, I think anywhere on shore is better than on board ship.

We arrived here early on Sunday morning and I came on shore and up here at daylight and, after enjoying a bath and a good breakfast, went to Bycullah Church in the morning. The same Chaplain officiated who was there when I first came to Bombay and I saw many faces that I knew, though the church was by no means full as people were reading their home letters.

I go on again the day after tomorrow in the *Columbian*, and we shall probably reach Galle on Sunday. It is quite wonderful how frequently Sunday happens to be the day or the morning of leaving or arriving.

I am now writing in a little bit of a room with bare walls such as you would hesitate to use as a scullery in England, and separated from the next by only a canvas screen. The furniture consists of a thing with four legs, called by courtesy a bed, another four-legged affair with a basin and a plate on top of it, a table and a chair. For this, I shall be charged perhaps half as much again as for the luxurious accommodation of the Grand Hotel at Paris. Such is the luxury of the East in the crack hotel of Bombay, and when you add to this the very pleasant smell which one gets from the main drain at night, you will say that it is quite time that the Oriental Hotels Co. did something.

October 16th

Early this morning we walked down to the new Dockyard in course of construction for the P&O Co. When it is finished they will have a splendid establishment here, but it will be a long while before either the Dock or workshops can be ready.

Breakfasted at the Club, and in the morning called on Captain Black and also on his wife. They are living in our old house, "The Rock", and it reminded me very much of old times to go there.

October 20th, at Galle

We have had a long and tedious passage down. The ship *Columbian* never was a clipper, and she is now very foul and her boilers out of order so that she positively won't go. We were stopped for some hours from the boilers giving out, and the last two days we have had very boisterous rough weather; however, we have lots of room and a very good table and so made ourselves very happy, knowing that on account of the breakdown of the steamer on the home side we shall have to wait a little while here. We shall have to be ready to start at an hour's notice, as the *Nubia* may have to make a fast passage down and make up for delays. I am afraid we shall be late in arrival at Singapore, but it can't be helped.

I have been reading Kingslake's "Crimea" on the way down and have got about halfway through it. It is very interesting but very plain-spoken, particularly as regards the Emperor of the French. I had no idea before reading it of all that took place in Paris at the election of the present Emperor.

October 24th

I have just time to say that we are off this afternoon in the *Columbian* again. I will write again from Singapore.

November 3rd, at Singapore

I am just able to write you a line by the French steamer which leaves immediately to announce our safe arrival here this morning after a somewhat tedious passage. I am going to stay a fortnight here.

November 7th

I have safely progressed thus far, although not quite as speedily as I had expected, for a combination of causes delayed the arrival of the mail three or four day: first the breakdown of the *Poonah* on the home side, next the carrying away of part of the Egyptian railway by the overflow of the Nile, and last the low rate of speed at which it is possible to drive the old *Columbian*. There has been a survey on the ship here, and it has been decided that the boilers are in too shaky a condition to make it prudent for her to go up the China Sea against the strong monsoon which is blowing now, and they have decided upon sending her back to Bombay with this mail and turning the China steamer, *Emeu*, which arrived yesterday, back again to Hong Kong, with *Columbian's* mails and passengers. I am afraid this will be the cause of a good deal of growling against the P&O, as people naturally say, why was the ship sent from Bombay with her boilers in such bad condition? She certainly will not be able to make another voyage till she has her new engines and boilers which are coming out for her, but it will be a long while before they can be got in, as they have their hands full in Bombay for some months to come.

The Company are laying out a Dockyard there which, when complete, will be a splendid place and they will be able to do any amount of work there as readily and almost as well as it could be done in England.

The *Columbian*, although not fast, is a comfortable vessel and we had a very pleasant voyage up. I had a cabin that I might have had a quadrille party in. It would hold all my luggage comfortably and we had lots of ice and a very good table, so we were not so badly off.

145

I have been quite received with open arms here and most people say they wish I could stop. So do I, but it is not to be. The Governor sent down to ask me to go up to dinner there directly he heard of my arrival, and I am already engaged somewhere every night that I am likely to be here.

I am going out to stay at Murray's today. Our old house is pulled down and the place looks quite desolate. They have begun to rebuild it but are getting on very slowly. Macaulay has taken a house about a couple of miles away from New Harbour, till the old place is built up again. He received me in a very kind and friendly manner and gave me a cordial welcome, but I think we shall probably be better friends apart than together. I don't believe he will remain long here, and if he does not, I shall try very hard to be sent back.

His wife is a pretty little woman, very shy and reserved and, I should fancy, with not much mind but not deficient in matter, or rather, means. Her father is a wealthy man and Macaulay gets some money with her, some say £10,000, and will have more when the old man dies. She has never been more than twenty or thirty miles out of Melbourne before, knows nothing of England and thoroughly detests and abominates Singapore. I can hardly wonder at her not liking it as it appears that she knows very few people, for hardly any of the ladies have called upon her because he would call on no-one when he came. Few people like Singapore, or indeed any place out here, at first and it must be very slow work for her to be left at home alone all day with no-one to talk to and a pack of native servants who can't understand what she says to them.

My two little dogs are flourishing and I intend to take them on to China, much to the distress of the persons who have had charge of them.

November 14th

I will not let you be a mail behind without a line to say that I am thankful to say all is well and I am going on to Hong Kong tomorrow morning after a pleasant and very flattering reception in old Singapore.

I am quite tempted to wish that I might remain here, but Macaulay has promised that if he goes away, to recommend me for the Agency, and I think it is quite within the verge of possibility that a few months may see me down here again. I am persuaded that such a move would give unqualified satisfaction to the good folks of Singapore.[3]

November 23rd, on board *Orissa*

Never before within the memory of the oldest inhabitants of the *Orissa* has she kicked and plunged about to such an extent as since we left Singapore. We have been coming up against the strength of the N.E. monsoon which is blowing unusually strongly, and the consequence is that our passage, which in a fair monsoon would not take more than five days, will occupy about eleven. It is a great thing, under such circumstances, to be in such a supremely comfortable vessel as the *Orissa* is. In such a craft as the *Vectis*, for example, such weather would be almost unbearably miserable. As it is, the old vessel rolls and pitches about in a way that makes landsmen very unhappy generally. As far as I am concerned, I have my sea legs on me pretty well, never having felt the least inclination to be sick since I left the *Vectis*, and as we have a number of pleasant people on board, and have lots of room and a capital table, there is not much to grumble about.

I am sorry you had to pay extra for my letters from France. They were stamped at the Hotels and I trusted to the fools there putting on stamps enough.

My little dogs are well and are on board with me. We have had a great deal of fun with them as they and a pet goat, belonging to the ship, on board are deadly enemies and the goat is very much afraid of them. He is one of those good-tempered animals only to be found on board ship. He will beg, salaam and lie dead like a clever dog, and his favourite record is a sheet of paper or a cigar, either of which he will eat with much gusto, but he is not very particular: gunny-bags, rope-ends, white trousers and paper collars are all very acceptable to him. He is very jealous of there being any other pets on board and butts at the little dogs, while they dart at him.

We have about 150 Beloochee troops on board, the wildest set of ragamuffins you ever saw. They are an irregular corps and have only one officer belonging to a native sepoy regiment in charge of them. They are far more powerful and more plucky men than the Southern Indians and are very fond of fighting. The rows that they have among themselves are something fearful sometimes, and they are very difficult to keep in order. Fortunately since we left Singapore they have nearly all been sea sick and not able to do much mischief, but they had a great deal of trouble with them in calm weather. As an instance of what they are, one night a number of them were sent to sleep below, on the orlop deck, and one of them dropped something which they couldn't find in the dark, so what should they do but collect together all the remains of their ghee (rancid butter) into a big dish and set alight to it. The consequence was a tremendous flare up, which put the officers of the watch in a great stew, thinking the ship must be on fire. They are up to all sorts of tricks, too. One of them the other day pretended

147

to be dying because he wanted some flour instead of rice to eat. They offered him some bread, which he would not have, and because he could not get what he wanted he ran to the side and threatened to throw himself overboard. His officer kicked him forward and in ten minutes he was as well as could be.

NOTES
   1. Kensal Green is one of the great Victorian cemeteries.
   2. It remains the practice on P&O passenger ships for the Captain to conduct a form of service on Sunday mornings, a privilege rarely delegated to clergymen.
   3. Kendall did not return to Singapore.

7 The South Eastern Railway's new packet *Victoria*, 1861.

8
At Hong Kong

November 30th, 1863

Here I am at last. The *Orissa* got in about nine a.m. on Thursday and I came on shore at once.

To my surprise I find that Sutherland has no advice whatever about me, good or bad or indifferent. No-one has sent him a line and the question of pay, position and everything else is quite open. I am therefore quite unable at present to settle down to anything or even to make any personal arrangements as to living, etc. I am at present staying with Capt. Caldbeck, who is an old friend. Sutherland would have taken me in, but he has young Allan staying with him, and so his spare room is occupied.

I like Sutherland much. He is a thorough gentleman, as well as being a very clever man and good man of business. He is a man eminently given to hospitality, and will have everything in the best possible style. His dinners are a by-word in Hong Kong. I am not quite sure that he does not perhaps a little overdo it, but in such a style-seeking place as Hong Kong is, you must do things well if you want to hold your own.

I can imagine nothing more delightful than the climate here just now. The sun is powerful enough in the middle of the day to require a puggery or even an umbrella but still the air is cool.

I am glad to hear that old Sinclair has got back to England safely and that he is all the better for his trip.

My little dogs, Tom and Jennie, are very well, but like a flannel jacket to sleep under this weather.

December 12th

At the present I am like a fish out of water, as I have to attend office some part of the day, for form's sake, but have nothing to do, except pick up notions of my own account, and vary the monotony of the day by going out to call somewhere.

Hong Kong as a place improves on acquaintance, at least at this season of year. The climate is most delightful, and there seem to be a number of pleasant people here, though they say that there are some who give themselves great airs, and that cliqueisms and jealousies are rife. The P&O

149

as a rule take a far higher standing here than they do anywhere else in the East. This is to a great extent Sutherland's doing, and as he has always had some good men with him since he has been in charge of the Agency, he has been able to maintain a good standard, although as regards pay we are worse off than probably another set of men, holding any position at all, as Mercantile men.

Sutherland is, without doubt, the right man in the right place. He takes a liberal and practical view of everything and withal managing to keep on good terms with all the mercantile and official world, is yet a capital manager of the Company's business as one will often meet with. I have always said since I knew him that I considered him the best man whom the Company have out here, and the more I know him, the more my opinion is confirmed and strengthened. The difference between him and Macaulay is very striking, though I believe them both to be honestly doing their duty as the Company's servants to the best of their ability. The one is liberal and comprehensive in his ideas, affable in his manners and with all the points of a thorough gentleman, as well as man of business about him; the other is a priggish little dandy who always makes himself disliked, wherever he goes, and who is one of the most narrow-minded sticklers for red tape that I ever met with. At the same time there is much about him that one cannot help liking but he is so insufferably eaten up with self-conceit that I believe he thinks there can be no-one in the world equal to himself, unless it may be Mr. Ritchie, whom he has always made his model, as far as he could, even to imitating the peculiar noise which he used to make in cleaning his teeth of a morning. For myself, I have no doubt that all will turn up trumps somehow in the end, and if I have to serve under anyone, I would sooner do so under Sutherland than anyone else, out here.

Sutherland would have asked me to stay with him at first, but young Allan was with him and was occupying his only furnished spare room. He went away by the last mail, and is going on to Calcutta and afterwards to Australia before going home. He is a pleasant quiet lad, very like both his father and mother.

The houses here are much better finished than any one sees in India or the Straits. They have to be built both for cold and hot weather, so that they have to be good substantial houses; at the same time the rooms are large and high. Sutherland's house is a very good one, containing on the ground floor three large rooms, one of which is the dining room, one the study or writing room and the other will be the billiard room, when he gets a table. Upstairs a large and handsomely-furnished drawing room, and three large bedrooms, with

150

bathroom, etc., attached. One can hardly help thinking that one is in a handsome room in England, sitting as one does of an evening in a well-carpeted room with curtains drawn before a blazing fire.

One great item of expense here is house rent. For Sutherland's house, which you will say is not a very large one, the rent is $2,000, or about £450 a year, besides taxes. For the Caldbecks' house, which consists of only four rooms and a store closet, the rent is £225 a year. So you see that if a person has to pay house rent out of a moderate income, it does not leave much for pin money. With us we are all supposed to be found quarters of some sort by the Company, and I suppose that if I should not continue to stay with Sutherland I shall find somewhere or another a place to lay my head. Indeed Caldbeck has asked me to come and live with them, but I do not think I shall do so. Time will shew.

December 14th

Our eyes were gladdened by the sight of the English mail signal yesterday morning, Sunday of course. Her delay was due to the *Mooltan* from Suez having broken down and being detained some time on the voyage to repair damages.

There was a large farewell party given a day or two after my arrival by a Mrs. Still who is going home this mail. Sutherland procured an invitation for me and I spent a very pleasant evening. There were fifty-nine ladies present! A wonderful gathering for Hong Kong, though we could beat it at Singapore. I, of course, knew but few ladies but I went in for dancing and managed to secure six, at which I considered myself very fortunate, particularly as I did not go till late and it is the fashion to engage dances beforehand.

I have not yet seen the Bishop. I called there one day and left Mr. Selwyn's note, and am invited to a teastruggle there tomorrow night. He, the Bishop, is going home again in a month or two. I find that he is very unpopular here: one can hardly find anyone with a good word to say for him. They say he is very conceited and lazy and never at his work. These last two I think must be in a great measure put down to ill health for there is no doubt that he has been a sufferer for some years. He is certainly by no means a stirring preacher and I don't think the Colonial Chaplain, Mr. Irwin who is an old man, is much more so. Last Sunday, a young East Coast missionary preached and gave us some startling doctrines about the millennium.

I went some days ago with Mrs. Townsend to call on Mrs. Gaynor and spent over an hour at Kowloon with her. They are living at Kowloon, the

151

opposite side of the harbour to the town of Victoria, about three quarters of an hour by boat from the P&O office. There is I think only one other lady besides Mrs. Gaynor over there, so she must find it rather lonely. It is a regular kind of camp or picnic life. They have a little bit of a bungalow, built of boards and straw, and divided into two, or perhaps three, rooms. There is no-one at present near them but soldiers as it is too far off from Hong Kong for people to go to for a permanent residence, that is to say if they have any business in Hong Kong and, then again, sometimes it blows so hard that there can be no communication for perhaps two or three days. I am afraid that while they are living over at Kowloon, I shall not be able to see as much of them as I should like. It is something like a person living over at Priddy's Hard, Gosport, and no means of getting over there except taking a boat the whole way.

This is a very different place to Singapore in many ways. Business is carried on in quite a different manner, approximating perhaps more nearly to the manner of doing things in Bombay and Calcutta, but different again to them. There is a man called a Compradore, who receives and pays all cash, sometimes having as much as $100,000 to $200,000 in his possession. These are generally men who have such an interest in the colony that it would not pay them to embezzle, but one does occasionally hear of such a thing. The P&O Compradore is one of the wealthiest men in the place, and is said to be worth at least three millions sterling. Twenty or thirty years ago he was a common coolie.

Everyone seems to have been making money in the East this last year; in fact it has been just the year of all others for turning over the dollars and I have been out of the way of it. I am afraid that the game is nearly played out now, but there may yet be a chance of doing something. I prefer, however, going cautiously to work, particularly in a new place. I have already gone into a venture which I hope will put £150 to £200 in my pocket, within the next day or two, and if it turns out as well as I have every reason to expect, I cannot but consider it fortunate. If I had been here three months sooner, I might have been $5,000 or $6,000 richer than I am now, from one thing alone. However, it is no use crying over spilt milk, and I must only suppose that it is better for me that I was not here, and that if it is good for me I may yet be able to turn over an honest dollar or two.

Sutherland is a very shrewd man, at the same time a very scrupulous one. I expect he has made a good deal of money one way and another. I hope he may be able to help me towards putting something in my pocket, as I want something to fill up the hole which my trip to England made, a good big one you may believe, but still the pleasure of being at home and seeing you all again was worth a great deal more.

You will have heard from the papers that the *Alabama* has found her way out here.[1] My only wonder is that she never came before. She is now somewhere about the Straits of Sunda and has already burnt three ships. The *Wyoming* United States war steamer was at Singapore at the date of last despatches from there and they expected that the *Alabama* would shortly look in there. Indeed, there was a little bit of excitement the other day there as the *Wyoming* was going in. There was a steamer called the *Indore* going into port at the same time, and the *Wyoming* ran down to her to board her. The two ships were close together, blowing off steam, and could be distinctly made out from some of the merchants' offices. People mistook the steam for the smoke of guns and made sure that the *Wyoming* and *Alabama* were having a set to outside. Both Singapore and Hong Kong are full of American ships, which are naturally unable to get employment.

The accounts from Japan are conflicting and rather uncertain, but I think that things look on the whole more peaceable.[2] They say that Satsuma is likely to come to terms and that we shall maintain our footing in that country. People write much more confidently from Kanagawa, and perhaps one of the best practical arguments in favour of peace is that trade is reviving and the exploit of silk continued on a large and increasing scale.

It is disheartening to find how Chinese servants break things. They are even worse than the natives of India and such a set of thieves and rascals as the whole race of Chinamen are, with some few wealthy exceptions, it would be difficult to find in any other part of the world. I find that it is the exception for a person not to sleep, even in Hong Kong, with a loaded revolver under his pillow for, although doors and windows are locked and bolted, they manage to break in frequently at night time, and they have some peculiar kind of pastille that they burn which is apt to send anyone in the room, even a dog, into a deep sleep. They are very adroit and very daring and one is never safe from them. Robbery with violence is very common where their numbers exceed those of the party attacked, but I never heard of a Chinaman attacking a European single-handed. They will rob you in any way they can.

In India, there is honour among thieves, and by keeping a rascal of a ramoosie, you are supposed to pay blackmail and to be pretty safe, but here they will steal from one another as soon as they will take from you. Taking Chinamen as a whole, I abominate them, and yet they are a wonderful people. Many of them are industrious, thrifty and clever but, as a rule, they

153

are great rascals, but what can you expect of men who wear tails and women who wear trousers?

There are no carriages and in this weather one can walk and enjoy it. In the summer, one is dependent on chairs.

January 1st, 1864

Last mail brought out no instructions from home either to or about me, so that I am still in the dark as to what I am to do, but Sutherland is so kind and considerate and treats me so well that I feel the anomaly of my position less probably than I should with anyone else.[3]

You will see that the "Mercenary Fleet", or "Buttons", as they are irreverently termed out here, of Sherard Osborn have been altogether dispersed.[4] Nearly the whole of the ships have been sent back to England to be sold, the best thing that could be done with them, I fancy.

The presence of the *Alabama* in these parts has put the hottest Northerners into such a state of trepidation that all the coasting steamers trading under the American flag, of which there are a good many in these waters, are changing their colours and coming out as Britishers. For American vessels proper, no employment whatever can be obtained. There are a good many Americans in Hong Kong, mostly of course Northerners, and one family carry their *esprit de pays* so far that they will not see English people at all. Others are more liberal and charitable but there is one instance here of a Northern husband and Southern wife, and they naturally don't talk politics much at home.

There was a large party here the other day at the Club and I happened to be dancing a gallop with a very jolly American lady, a Mrs. Burrows. Not thinking particularly of what I was saying, I remarked what a capital gallop it was, it was certainly the best of the evening. "Oh yes, Dixie's Land," she said quietly, and I was shut up.

News from Japan is apparently better. Satsuma has paid the indemnity and has promised to do his utmost to trace and punish Mr. Richardson's murderers.

NOTES

1. The American Civil War dragged on and Palmerston and Russell wisely maintained British neutrality. Russell acted too late to stop a newly-built ship, *Alabama*, from sailing from Liverpool in August 1862 under the Confederate flag and then proceeding to sink a great amount of Northern shipping until her capture and sinking two years later.

2. In attempting to maintain a closed border policy, the Japanese caused much resentment

among foreign governments. Richardson, a British merchant in Yokohama, was murdered by a retainer of the Lord of Satsuma who refused to hand the man over to the British. The affair ended with the British seizing three Japanese ships and, later, bombarding the forts of Kagoshima.

3. Kendall was posted to Calcutta in March 1864 and then to Bombay in the following October. In January 1865, he was posted to Melbourne where he remained until his return to the London office in 1881.

4. Captain Sherard Osborn RN served with distinction in the Chinese and Crimean Wars. In 1852, he commanded one of the Franklin search expeditions and, in 1858, navigated the Yangtse as far as Hangkow. In 1862, he accepted a request from the Chinese government to command a squadron of six ships specially fitted out in England to suppress piracy on the coast of China. It had been agreed that he would take his orders from the Imperial Government but, on his arrival in 1863, he found that his fleet would be under the command of the Mandarins. Foreseeing problems, he gave up his appointment and returned to England with those officers who had joined him.

8 Satsuma's envoys paying the indemnity for the murder of Mr. Richardson, 1864.

Menu.

Huîtres.

POTAGE.

Consommé Monte Carlo.   Velouté Princesse.

POISSON

Filets de Sole Daglieré.   Blanchailles.

ENTRÉE

Vol-au-vent à la Toulouse.

RELEVÉ.

Selle de Mouton Richelieu.

Choux de Bruxelles.   Pommes Châteaux.

Sorbet Veuve Clicquot

RÔTI

Chapon en Cocotte.   Salade de Saison.

Jambon d'York, Braisé aux Xérès.

Épinards au Jus.

ENTREMETS.

Soufflé au Curaçoa.   Gelée aux Fruits.

Bombe Nesselrode.

Petits Fours Assortis.

Dessert.   Café.

Programme.

Toast   -   -   "The King."
Proposed by THE CHAIRMAN.
The National Anthem.

SONG ...   "The Charmed Cup"   ...   *Reichel*
Mr. EDGAR COYLE

SONGS { (a) "Love hath Echoes" }   ...   *Liddle*
{ (b) "Love's Philosophy" }
Mr. THOMAS THOMAS

HUMOROUS SONG ... "The Last Straw"...   *Braham*
Mr. JAMES GODDEN.

Toast   -   -   "Our Guest."
Proposed by THE CHAIRMAN.

SONG ...   "The Pipes of Pan"   ...   *Elgar*
Mr. IVOR FOSTER.

SONG ...   "My Queen"   ...   *Blumenthal*
Mr. WALTER HYDE.

HUMOROUS RECITATION by
Mr. W. G. CHURCHER.

Response   -   -   Mr. F. R. KENDALL.

SONG...   "Marie, My Girl"   ...   *Aitken*
Mr. EDGAR COYLE.

SONG ...   "Roses"   ...   *Adams*
Mr. THOMAS THOMAS.

HUMOROUS SONG ... "I World"   ...   *Stanhope*
Mr. JAMES GODDEN.

Toast   -   -   "The Chairman."
Proposed by Mr. H. J. TAYLOR.

SONG...   "Glorious Devon"   ...   *Ed. German*
Mr. IVOR FOSTER.

SONG...   "A Wand'ring Minstrel" (Mikado)...   *Sullivan*
Mr. WALTER HYDE.

Response   -   -   CAPTAIN P. HARRIS.

HUMOROUS RECITATION by
Mr. W. G. CHURCHER.

AT THE PIANO   -   Mr. F. R. KINKEE.

---

9 Programme of a Dinner given at the Great Eastern Hotel on 20th February 1906 to celebrate the 50th year of F.R. Kendall's service with P&O.

9

At Bombay again

January 13th, 1865 [1]

We have been anxiously expecting the English mail for the last day or two, and as she has not come in, I have no letter of yours to acknowledge today. I suppose she will turn up tomorrow, but as we know that she burnt a boiler out going up to Suez, we are not anxious at her non-appearance.

There has been very little to disturb the even tenor of our existence during the past fortnight, the usual amount of gambling and speculation on the share market, but I have neither time nor money to devote to such things and think it only right to be very careful in all my dealings just now. Bombay is in a very unpleasant stage of progression at present, that is for all who are not making fortunes, inasmuch as the great tendency of all unchecked speculation is to put prices up and so affect all people with moderate fixed incomes to an alarming extent.

We had a shipwreck the other morning in sight of the house. A large vessel called the *Sydenham* trying to cut the corner a little too sharply ran on the rocks and is a total wreck. Fortunately it was a fine calm night, and there were no lives lost. A week before there was a large fire in the Fort which thoroughly burnt out our old office, so that we should have had a roasting if we had remained in our old quarters.

May 12th

There is not a great deal of news here, except that in the way of business, everything is in a kind of collapse. If there is not actually a panic, there is such a complete want of confidence that shares and stocks of all kinds are unsaleable and everybody is hard up. The fact is, people have been gambling to a fearful extent really, and literally gambling with or without money, no matter. Everyone could get credit and as long as things kept rising and the market was firm, all went merry as a marriage bell. Suddenly and unexpectedly, the telegraph brings news from England and America eminently disastrous to the cotton interests. There is a general desire to realise and confidence collapses immediately.[2]

Long heads are now calmly and carefully considering the matter with a view to making some arrangements under which justice may as far as possible be done to everyone, and widespread ruin which was staring nearly everyone in the face may be somewhat averted. Large fortunes have been made in Bombay the last two or three years with marvellous ease, and they are dissipated with just as remarkable rapidity. Many men who were two months ago considered millionaires are now most hopelessly involved beggars. Happy the man who has realised and cleared out of it in time.

It was really ludicrous to hear bits of boys just come out as juniors in banks, talking of lakhs as if they were nothing at all.[3] No-one was considered to have done anything at all unless he could talk of two lakhs to his credit. Now it is, "By Jove, I stand to lose so much, how much do you?" Personally, I have had very little to do with shares from the simple reason that I have not had money and would not trade on borrowed capital, or rather speculate with it in shares. The consequence is that though I must lose a little money if things continue as they are now, I can at any rate pay my way, and I hope to make enough in other ways to compensate for anything I may have lost.

But you will not care about a letter which is simply a money article, and so I will go on to other things.

First to tell you of a serious and inconvenient loss which I met with last Sunday coming home from morning church. It was a fearfully hot day and the sun was even more powerful than usual. Coming up over the hill, one of my horses tottered and fell down. We threw cold water over his head and got him out of harness as quickly as possible and at last got him on his feet and let him walk quietly up the hill, but the poor brute never reached home, he died on the road. I can account for his death in no other way than by supposing that he was knocked over by the heat. All the poor horses in Bombay are feeling the weather and there is scarcely one in Bombay that is not afflicted with mange or something of the kind.

I believe we are to lose Captain Black very soon, though nothing definite is known yet, even by himself, I believe, except that he is going home and is to be relieved by Captain Henry.[4] Captain Henry is undoubtedly a good man, but a man without the remotest idea of business, I fancy. This does not much matter as long as he is well supported and, as he is an old friend of mine, I daresay we shall get on very well together.

We had a grand dinner at the Town Hall the other night, a farewell to Mr. Anderson, one of our leading civilians. About one hundred sat down and we had some of the best speeches I have heard for a long time. Sherard Osborn was there and spoke. It is the first time I have seen him since I was introduced to him at 21, Bedford Place, when he was a young Lieutenant and I a little blue. *Tempora mutantur*!

I have been proposed as a member of the Asiatic Society which will also put me into the Bombay Geographical Society, and they have lately put me on the Committee of the Sailors' Home so that I hope to be able to make myself a little more useful than I have hitherto been.

They have had a terrible explosion at Singapore which if it had happened a few hours later would have proved fatal to nearly all the leading men of the place. A little steam yacht, lately brought out for the Tumongong, burst her boilers and blew up, killing or seriously hurting nearly everyone on board. A few hours later, she was to have started for a pleasure trip with the Governor and all the officials and principal men. The loss of life would then have been terrific; as it is, five Europeans and about sixteen or twenty natives have been killed. I have seen a photograph of the vessel after the explosion and such a scene I never saw; the inside of the vessel seems to be completely blown out.

July 7th

I wish I had a little more time to devote to calling and making the acquaintance of ladies, but I shall no doubt manage it gradually, and I fully intend during this rainy season to run up to Poonah for a day or two, if it is only for a little relaxation and change of air and scene.

We have the rainy season fully set in now and are thoroughly enjoying feeling a little cool again. This last summer has been the hottest ever known, they say, nearly all over India and I certainly never felt heat like it before. Bombay has been most alarmingly unhealthy through it, as such a filthy, beastly place as it is, must necessarily be, but now with the rain our sanitary condition is very much improving. Cholera, fever, dysentery, all the most dreaded Eastern diseases have been rife and it is only within the last week or two that the mortality statistics have returned to something like their average rate.

It is curious to notice how comparatively free Europeans are from epidemic diseases, simply and solely because of their greater cleanliness, and their liking for fresh air. The grandest native house in the place is a pig sty; you wouldn't think perhaps that many of the European ones were much better, so shabby are they, but the first thing that a rich native does with his house is to case it round with glass, so as to make a gigantic hot-house of it, and shut out every atom of fresh air. Then their habits and manners are enough to make any moderately squeamish Englishman sick. Pen and ink cannot describe the filth and stinks of the bazaar, the great native town. I really think it gets worse and worse every year. I would back certain parts of Bombay to vie with any other place in the world for the number and variety of its stinks.

It is all very well for Dr. Livingstone to say they are wholesome; they may be, but they are anyhow not pleasant. Things are permitted in Bombay, too, that would be allowed in no other place under British rule. It is enough to allude to the Parsee Towers of silence where the dead are exposed on racks till the vultures have picked them clean; the sight and smell of roasting Hindus are not pleasant, but are I suppose less objectionable from a sanitary point of view.[5]

What I object to principally in the way of dealing with the dead is that with all the lower classes the bodies are carried on biers, with all the features perfectly exposed, probably painted, and the old head wagging about in a most ghastly and inhuman-looking manner. Others again are propped up in tonjon chairs and carried along in this manner just as if they were alive. The sight is not pleasant, and to ladies might often be fatal. I always long to whip every member of a funeral procession such as this, and would do so frequently were it not for the respect one feels for the presence of death. Do the police trouble themselves to put nuisances of this sort down? No. Do the Municipal Commissioners prosecute them for a breach of the Conservancy Act? No. Nobody appears to think it is his business to do anything for the good of the place. Europeans are too apathetic, too much occupied in making money and thinking how soon they can shake off the last Bombay dust on the deck of a P&O steamer. Natives accept nuisances as matters of course. They don't feel annoyed by them, and would not think of lifting a little finger to abate one of them.

I saw an article in the "Saturday Review" not long since, speaking of Calcutta as the filthiest of cities. It is a perfect paradise of cleanliness as compared with Bombay, and had we the Calcutta climate here with no sea breezes, this place would be simply unbearable.

September 25th

I started for Poona after the last mail had gone away and enjoyed three days there very much. I had never been so far up the railway before and was much delighted with the beautiful scenery of the ghauts.

I suppose that the Bhore Ghaut Railway Incline is one of the most remarkable, if not the most, piece of railway engineering in the world. The ascent is about forty-five miles long and the gradient is one inch in fifty or less. The tunnels, of which there are several, are all hewn out of the solid rock and the peeps of scenery which one gets are as varied as they are charming. The effect is considerably heightened just now at the close of the rainy season, by numbers of cascades which jump and tumble about from rock to rock for hundreds of feet above and below. The railway occasionally runs so near the edge of precipice that it makes one to shudder to look out of the window. About midway up the ghaut there is a reversing station, an absolute necessity I imagine in so steep an incline of such length, whence, after stopping long enough for the engines to take water, you start again in the opposite direction and are surprised to look out of the window and find the second half of the train. A train is always divided before ascending or descending the incline, toiling its way up the slope one hundred or one hundred and fifty feet below you and apparently right underneath. So near is it that you might throw a glass of water on the top of the carriages as they pass.

The air appears wonderfully different as soon as one gets well on the ghauts. It feels not only much cooler but so much cleaner and purer than the plains and, as we rushed on from Khandalla at the top of the ghauts to Poona, it seemed positively cold.

All the Bombay world and his wife have been at Poona during the rains and there has been a great deal of gaiety going on: balls, parties, picnics, races, fancy fairs, etc., etc., etc., following one another in rapid succession. I went one day to the races, where one goes rather for the sake of seeing people than horse-racing, the latter being poor enough, and I was at a concert one evening. We rode too out to Parbullee, about five miles off, an old ruined castle on the top of a high hill whence old Teroze watched the Battle of Kirkee and saw the end of his raj.[6]

Coming down from Poona, we had a good deal of detention on the railway; a huge stone had tumbled down across the rails on the ghaut, and we were detained about four hours at one station in consequence.

September 27th

I see by a stray paper which came in yesterday, that you were to have grand doings at the R.N.C. on the occasion of the French Fleet being at Portsmouth and I have been wondering whether you will have been at home and in the thick of it or whether you will have been still in the north with the Richardsons.

January 13th, 1866

The first letter written to you this year, my dearest Mother, and it takes with it all good wishes for the year that we have just entered in. We have all of us much to be thankful for in the blessings of the past year; with myself I feel that I have special reason to be grateful for being spared so long in health and comfort.

We have just completed one of the most trying years that Bombay has ever known, both in climate and commercial matters. I have been spared from serious illness of any kind and if not much richer in pocket than I was at the commencement of the year, I am not at any rate completely ruined, as very many friends around me are.

The *Malta* had hardly left the harbour with last mails when the *Baroda* was signalled. Dr. Livingstone and I went on board together to meet Lady Franklin and I was a little disappointed when I got alongside not to see old Sinclair's eager face among the many peering over the side at us.[7]

I was very warmly welcomed by Lady Franklin and Miss Cracroft and when they told me that the question of Sinclair's coming or not had been entirely left for their asking, I was by no means surprised that they had not made the request. I am by no means surprised at Lady Franklin not wanting him for an escort. She is an old traveller and knows that ladies travelling by themselves are always well looked after, whereas if they have a gentleman with them, it is supposed to be his business to attend upon them and, unless he knows the places, etc., he may often be not so useful as an utter stranger. Then again, wherever Lady Franklin goes, she will not want for attention, and I think she was perhaps afraid of being put to some expense on Sinclair's account, which she certainly would have been if he had travelled about in India with her.

Everyone here thinks it an extraordinary plucky thing for an old lady of her age to attempt such a journey as she is making. By the bye, do you know exactly what her age is? She must I think be over 70.[8] It is, I hear currently reported in Bombay, that her object in coming here is to consult Sherard Osborn as to the practicability and advisability of sending another Arctic expedition, and the fact of Sherard Osborn being about to run home quickly in six weeks' time will rather strengthen popular opinions, as folks will be certain to say that he is gone home on her urgings to set another expedition on foot. She is quite the heroine of the day in Bombay.

On New Year's Day, we all dined at Government House, Malabar Point, a quiet little party of twelve. I have been escorting them about as well as I could of an afternoon after office and we have done the best we could to make them feel comfortable and at home. One day we went on a picnic to Elephanta and had a peep at the caves, with which the ladies seemed much

162

interested. Captain Osborn had taken them out one day previously in a Government steamer, where they got no tiffin, but I think we made amends for that defect the day they went over in the *Colaba*.

The ladies left yesterday morning for Matheran where they intend to stay for two days, then go on to Poona, thence to Mahabaleshwar, and back again to Bombay. They will find it hard work, I think, but nothing seems to fatigue Lady Franklin. Osborne put a carriage at their disposal and gave them a Deputy Traffic Manager to escort them to Narel, with a free pass to and from any station on the line.

It is really quite a novel sensation, and I need hardly say a pleasurable one, to have ladies in the house. It takes one a little bit away from the selfish kind of boredom of bachelor life and makes one wish the proper person would turn up to take the other end of the table. Lady Franklin is so pleasant and kind and cheerful that one appreciates her presence all the more.

Several wealthy natives have been to pay their respects. To some of them she brought letters of introduction from that arch-humbug, Sir Manackjee Cursetjee, as the English papers dub him. I cautioned her to be a little careful of these as Manackjee doesn't altogether go down in Bombay, whatever he may do in England.[9]

We are to have some "Assemblies" here this year, dancing parties which are to be very nice and very select. I have been invited to subscribe and have done so, but there is not the same amount of sociability here that there is in Singapore, for instance, and though one may make one or two friends here and there, people do not cotton on to one another easily. Lady Frere's arrival will, I suppose, be the commencement of the gaiety.

Lady Franklin gave me the hint, and I think I have earned their lasting gratitude by taking them up to Malabar Hill and giving them some dinner and a little rest before they had to go on board the wretched little Kuerachee steamer.

Lady Franklin was just in time to catch Dr. Livingstone. He left on the third in the *Thule* for Zanzibar.[10] We drank him a pleasant voyage and Aunt Ellen's good health in the evening at dinner.

I really must not go on scribbling and will only add love to all dear ones and kindest regards to all friends. Ever, my dearest Mother,

Your affectionate son,

F. R. Kendall

NOTES

1. There is a gap of one year between this and the previous letter. Kendall came to Bombay, from a short posting in Calcutta, in October 1864.

2. The American Civil War had stopped the supply of raw cotton from the Southern States to Great Britain and much speculation then followed on the various markets. The submission of the Southern States in 1865 re-established the supply of cotton and prices fell as a result. One of the causes of the Stock Market crash in 1987 was said to be the speed with which newly-introduced computers signalled fluctuations in market supply and demand. Here, in the case cited by Kendall, is an early example of the potential effects of rapid communication (i.e., the Electric Telegraph).

3. A lakh is one hundred thousand rupees. One hundred lakhs makes one crore.

4. Captain George Fitzgerald Henry was was suspended for one voyage following the grounding of *Hindostan* at Suez in May 1856 (he was acting Commander) and was wrecked in the *Alma* in June 1859. Appointed Superintendent at Bombay in 1865, a position he held until his death in 1877. Henry Road in Bombay (still in existence) is named in his memory.

5. The Parsee Towers of Silence in Bombay are at the top of a hill, well away from public gaze and Hindu cremations are normally private affairs. While Kendall may have witnessed the sights described, he must have made a conscious effort to see them and, in these circumstances, he may be over-reacting.

6. In 1817, the three great Mahratta powers at Poona, Nagpur and Indore rose against the British. Elphinstone, then Resident at the Peshwa's court, had foreseen this and had ordered up a European regiment from Bombay. The Residence was burnt down and Kirkee attacked by the Peshwa's army which was repulsed. The Peshwa fled.

7. Dr. Livingstone left England in mid-August 1865 via Bombay with the object of suppressing slavery and finding the source of the Nile and arrived in Zanzibar on 20th January, 1866. He travelled to Zanzibar on Arthur Anderson's own private yacht, the *Thule*. Livingstone never returned to England and he was found dead on 1st May, 1873.

8. Lady Franklin was, in fact, 74 at this time and died in 1875, aged 83.

9. Manackjee Cursetjee was a Parsee philanthropist from Bombay. He corresponded regularly with Lord Elphinstone whom he addressed as "My respected friend". He wrote a lengthy letter to Parliament in 1853 recommending a "few passing ideas for the benefit of Indian and Indians".

10. It is likely that Dr. Livingstone was able to avail himself of a trip on *Thule's* delivery voyage to the Sultan of Zanzibar.

Vessels mentioned in Letters

(* indicates a non-P&O vessel)

Alabama* The British Government were too late to stop the newly-built steam sloop warship *Alabama* from sailing from Liverpool in August 1862 under the Confederate flag and proceeding to destroy over fifty Northern ships until her capture two years later. In June 1864, she entered Cherbourg followed by the Federal steamer *Kearsage*. In the offshore fight which followed, and which was watched by a large crowd, *Alabama* sank with the loss of 21 lives and 21 wounded.

Alhambra An iron screw barque with one funnel. Built in 1855. 729 gross tons, 10.5 knots. In July of 1857 she broke down off the Spanish coast and a rumour went round Southampton within the space of a few hours, long before news could possibly have been received. Sold to an Australian owner in 1862. Foundered off the Australian coast in 1888.

Alma Built in 1854, she was a 2,164-ton iron screw barque with one funnel. In June 1859 she was wrecked on a reef near the Hamish Islands, north of Perim. All hands and the mail were saved by H.M.S. *Cyclops* and the P&O *Nemesis*.

Argonaut* Built in Quebec for Graves in 1858, of 1,188 tons, she was in collision with *Madras* in 1861 (See entry for 21 October, 1861).

Australasian* Possibly the *Australian*, built in 1852 for the UK/India route. 735 tons.

Ava Built in 1855, the *Ava* was a single-funnelled iron screw barque of 1,373 gross tons and had a steam operated winch for cargo which was a great novelty at the time. While carrying women and children refugees from the Indian Mutiny in 1858, she was wrecked outside Trincomalee, her Captain having taken into account a current which, by some unfortunate freak, was not then running. Mails and a large part of the cargo were lost (including £250,000 worth of specie). No lives (including that of Lord Elgin) were lost. Captain Kirton, who was in command, was later appointed the Company Agent at Colombo and later served in Australia and Malta.

Bahiana* A cable-laying ship.

Baroda An iron screw brig with one funnel, built in 1864 of 1,874 tons. Sold in 1881.

Bee* Thought to be a small sailing boat owned by Kendall back in England.

Benares Built in 1858. An iron screw barque of 1,491 gross tons with one funnel. Wrecked, without loss of life, on an uncharted rock near Fisherman's Group in the China Seas in May 1868.

Bengal An iron screw barque of 2,185 gross tons, built in 1853. Nearly lost at Galle in June 1859 when struck by a squall at anchor and was driven ashore. Broke her shaft in 1863 and was towed into Aden by *Benares*. In 1864 she was grounded in the garden of the Bishop's College, Garden Reach, during a Calcutta cyclone and was salved after a canal had been cut for her. Broke her shaft in 1865. Sold in 1870 and wrecked near Java in 1885. When launched she was for some time the largest liner in the world and had a speaking tube to the Engine Room, regarded then as a great innovation.

Bombay The second ship to bear the name. Built in 1862, she was an iron screw barque with one funnel, of 1,186 tons. In 1861 she broke her new shaft near Penang and was towed to Singapore by *Mohr*. In 1862 she broke her shaft in the Indian Ocean and sailed to Mauritius where she fitted a spare. In 1870 she sank the U.S.S. *Oneida* in Yokohama with heavy loss of life. Sold in 1878 and destroyed by fire in 1880.

Candia Built in 1854. An iron screw barque with one funnel of 1,961 gross tons. In 1857

165

she was lengthened amidships and, in 1866, she was completely refitted and given new boilers. Served in 1874 in the Ashanti War and afterwards sold by auction. Bought by J. Howden of Glasgow who afterwards sold her to the Japanese, who renamed her *Wakanoura Maru*. Used as a store ship at Hokodate in 1896.

Chusan A steel screw barque with one funnel, built in 1852. 699 gross tons. In 1852, she was the first ocean-going steamer to make passage to Australia via the Cape on a regular service. She was sold to Hong Kong owners in 1861. In 1866 she was sold to the powerful and loyalist Choshu clan and, after conversion into a war ship, renamed *Kayo Maru*. The former *Chusan* was visited at her anchorage in Osaka by the Emperor Meiji, probably the first time that a Japanese Emperor had set foot aboard a Western ship. Broken up in 1870.

Colaba Probably the P&O *Colabah*, a 145-ton paddle tug completed in March 1863 for service at Calcutta but listed at Bombay by March 1863. Her engines were removed in 1882 and she was then used for a time as a lighter.

Columbian 2,283 gross tons. Bought by P&O in 1859 from the E&A Company. Sold in 1866 and, after having new engines fitted and other alterations and improvements, the P&O were so impressed with her they bought her back again the same year. Sold again to an Indian buyer in 1877 and was eventually broken up.

Cordelia* HMS *Cordelia*, a wooden steam sloop built in 1839, was on station in Australia at the time of Kendall's visit. She was sold in 1870.

Cyclops* In 1857, The Red Sea and India Telegraph Company was formed "with the view of establishing telegraphic communication from England to India by way of the Red Sea and eventually to China and Australia". H.M.S. *Cyclops*, a wooden paddle frigate built in 1839, was engaged in 1858 in making surveys and taking soundings "for the Electric Cable". She was sold in 1864.

Douro An iron screw barquentine of 810 gross tons, built in 1853. In May 1854 whilst en route from Hong Kong to Singapore, having met a terrific typhoon, she had her engines disabled and funnel carried away. She was completing her voyage under sail when she was blown onto the North Paracels Shoal in the China Sea and became a total loss. One life was lost. The Directors commended two officers who "proceeded, in a small open boat, from the place where the vessel was wrecked to Hong Kong, a distance of upwards of 300 miles, to obtain the assistance of some of the Company's other vessels, which they accomplished in a boisterous sea, by great exertion and risk".

Dunbar* The *Dunbar* was a ship of 1,321 tons and was wrecked on South Head at the entrance to Sydney Harbour in 1867. See notes.

Emeu An iron screw barque built in 1854 of 1,538 gross tons. Was originally an Atlantic liner until bought by P&O. Sold by auction in 1873, becoming a fully-rigged sailing vessel, and renamed *Winchester*. Wrecked in Straits of Magellan in 1880 but was salved and until 1898 was a hulk in China.

Erin Built in 1846, she was a wooden paddler of 979 gross tons with three masts and one funnel. In 1851 she collided with and sank the *Pacha*. In June 1857 she was wrecked at Caltura without loss of life, mail or specie.

Euxine An iron paddle brigantine with two funnels, built in 1847. 1,165 gross tons. Trooped to the Indian Mutiny in 1857. In 1869 she was sold and reconstructed by Lairds of Birkenhead as a sailing ship for Bates of Liverpool. Burned at sea in August 1874.

Fiery Cross* A tea clipper of 686 gross tons, built in Liverpool in 1855 for Campbell of Glasgow. Stranded in the China Sea in March 1860.

Fire Dart* An American ship. Details unknown.

Formosa Built in 1852, a screw barque of 675 gross tons. Chartered to the French Government in 1861 and sold to Chinese owners in 1871. Converted into a hulk in 1891.

166

Fort William P&O's coal and stores hulk in Hong Kong.

Ganges The second ship to bear the name. Built in 1850, sister ship to Singapore, she was an iron paddle barque of 1,190 gross tons with one funnel. Sold in 1871 to Chinese buyers and later broken up.

Granada A three-masted screw schooner of 561 gross tons, she was built in 1857. Saw Mauritius service in 1858 and was chartered by the Chinese Government in 1860 and to the French in 1861. Sold to Japan in 1866.

Great Eastern* Brunel's great ship, launched in 1857. 22,500 gross tons with a speed of 7.5 knots and 6,500 square yards of canvas sails, 6 masts, 4 funnels, a propeller and a paddle. Accommodation for 800 first class, 2,000 second class and 1,300 third class passengers. Stuck for three months at launching. An explosion while on trials killed six men and injured others. Purchased for work on the Atlantic for which she was not designed and made her first voyage with only 36 passengers. She lost most of her sails and smashed her paddles on her second voyage. Employed as a cable ship, laying the Atlantic cable in 1865. Moored in the Mersey as a showboat in 1886 and broken up in 1888.

Great Liverpool A wooden paddler of 1,311 gross tons, built in 1837 for Sir John Tobin and bought by P&O in 1838 for the Southampton to Alexandria run. Totally wrecked in February 1846 near Cape Finisterre with the loss of only two lives.

Great Western* Built by Brunel in 1838 for the Great Western Steamship Company for the new transatlantic service. Of 1,320 tons, she carried 128 first class and 20 second class passengers and a crew of 57.

Himalaya An iron screw steamer built in 1853. She was the largest and finest ship of her day. Was originally to have been a paddler but altered on the slips to screw. 3,438 gross tons, 13 knots. In 1854 it was realised that, with the increased cost of coal, she would be an uneconomic proposition and she was sold to the British Government for £130,000. She was used for trooping during the Mutiny and served well nearly up to the end of the century. It was *Himalaya* that carried Lord Cardigan, 700 men and 390 horses to the Crimea for the ill-fated Charge of the Light Brigade. Lord Cardigan's brother-in-law, rival and Commanding Officer, Lord Lucan, sailed for the Crimea in another P&O ship, *Simla*. Her figurehead was a fierce-visaged Himalayan warrior. Her end came in June 1940 when enemy planes sunk her at Portland where she was then serving as a coal hulk.

Indore* Details unknown.

Indus Built in 1847 and lengthened in 1852, Indus was 1,950 tons.

Iris* H.M.S. *Iris* had 26 guns and was based on the Australian station in 1859. She was launched at Pembroke in July 1840. Length 131 feet. In 1846 she saw service against the Borneo pirates. Lent to the Atlantic Telegraph Co. in 1865. Disappears from Navy Lists by 1871.

Lightning* Built in Boston in 1854 for Black Ball Line, *Lightning* was a wooden clipper of 2,096 tons, 244 feet long and spread 13,000 yards of canvas when under full sail. She was destroyed after catching fire when loading bales of wool in Geelong in October 1869. In March 1854, she sailed 436 miles in twenty four hours.

Linwood Possibly a "pet" name for the *Lady Mary Wood,* a 553-ton paddle steamer, one funnel. Bought in 1841 and sold in 1858.

Madras Built in 1852. An iron screw barque of 1,185 gross tons. In 1874, after being stranded at Nagasaki, sold to Japan. Laid up in 1896 and later wrecked.

Madrid An early iron paddler of 479 gross tons built in 1845. Two funnels, brig masted. In 1851 she brought Lajos Kossuth, the abdicated President of Hungary, to England. Wrecked on a sunken rock in Vigo Bay in February 1857 with no loss of life.

Malabar A screw brig of 917 gross tons built in 1858. Caught by a squall whilst anchored at Galle in May 1860, was driven ashore and wrecked carrying specie worth £287,740 and opium worth £100,000. Kipling, in his barrackroom ballad of "Trooping", wrote "The Malabar's in 'arbour and the Jumna's at her tail."

Malta An iron paddler, brig-rigged with two funnels of 1,217 gross tons, built in 1848. In 1858 she was lengthened at the bows and altered to screw. It was said that the place where her paddles had formerly been was always visible to the end. New gross tonnage, 1,942. Sold in 1878 and broken up in 1882.

Manila Bought by P&O in 1853. An iron screw barque of 646 gross tons. Transporting during the Crimean War. She was afterwards transferred to the Indian station where she trooped along the coast during the Mutiny, and was a refugee ship at Calcutta during the "Scare". Sold in 1860 and wrecked near Halifax in 1881.

Mazagon An 86-ton paddle steamer built for the Bombay Harbour service in 1858.

Mooltan One of the first steamers with steam-steering gear. Sold in 1881, had her engines removed and became the four-masted barque *Eleanor Margaret*. Reported missing in 1891.

Nemesis An iron screw full-rigged ship, built in 1857 of 2,018 gross tons. Was to have been named *Delhi* but name changed after the defeat of the Mutineers. Not very successful on the Eastern Service owing to her low ports, bad vents and unsatisfactory machinery. Given to Denny Bros. in 1873 in exchange for new engines for *Sumatra* and lengthened by them, making the gross tonnage 2,717. Finally broken up in 1890.

Norna An iron screw barque of 969 tons, built in 1853 for the Indian station. Trooped during the Crimean War. Broke her shaft off Trincomalee and sold to Hong Kong owners in 1864.

Northam An iron screw schooner of 1,330 gross tons, built in 1858. 12.5 knots. Grounded on a reef near Jeddah in August 1859 but salved. Sold to the Union Line for their Cape Services in 1870. Burned at sea in 1878. See Kendall's account of *Northam*'s accident.

Nubia Built in 1854, 2,096 gross tons, *Nubia* was an iron screw barque. In 1865 she was modernised in Bombay, having had new boilers fitted. In 1877 she was sold to the London School Board for £7,500 to become a training ship at Gray's and was renamed *Shaftesbury*. The cost of conversion and refurnishing was about £40,000. 3,763 boys were trained on her before it was decided to resell her, which was done in 1906 when £15,000 was still owing on her. She fetched £3,000.

Oneida* An iron screw steamer of 500 H.P. and 2,285 tons. Built in 1855 in Greenock and owned by the E&A Co in Glasgow.

Oriental A wooden paddler, built in 1840 of 1,787 gross tons. Was receiving and stores ship at Bombay from 1850 and was sold for scrap in 1861.

Orissa An iron screw barque of 1,647 tons. Launched in 1856 as *Franche Comtors* and bought by P&O that year. In 1860 she had a serious explosion on board. Sold in 1878 and converted into a sailing ship at Shanghai.

Ottowa A screw barque of 1,275 gross tons. Built in 1854 and one of the pioneer steam mail carriers to Canada. Transport in Crimea War. Bought by P&O in 1855 from the Allen Line. Broke her shaft in 1860. Sold to China in 1872.

Pacha Built in 1842, she was an iron paddler of 592 tons. Three masts and one funnel. Sunk in collision with the *Erin* in July 1851 with the loss of 16 lives in the Straits of Malacca.

Pekin Built in 1847, an iron paddler of 1,182 gross tons. She was brig-rigged with two funnels. She saw war service in the Crimea. In 1851 she came through a typhoon between Hong Kong and Singapore. Sold in 1867.

Pelonis* A British warship. Details unknown.

Poonah An iron screw barque, built in 1862 of 2,152 gross tons. In 1875 Blondin walked the tightrope between her main and mizzen masts at sea. In 1875 she was lengthened by 88 feet and had new engines fitted, her gross tonnage becoming 3,130. Afterwards her keel had a curious curve and, when dry-docking, the ship had to be specially blocked. Transport in Egyptian troubles in 1885/6. Sold in 1889 and broken up in Sunderland in 1892/3.

Pottinger Built in 1846, an iron paddle barque with two funnels. 1,401 gross tons until lengthened at the bows in 1849 when tonnage become 1,350. In 1846 she was stranded in fog in Thorness Bay, almost on top of the wreck of H.M.S. *Cyclops,* but refloated. Transporting in 1860 during the China disturbances. Sprang a leak in Bombay harbour in 1860 and had to be beached to prevent her sinking. Became a hulk in 1862 at Bombay and sold for scrap in 1867.

Rainbow* An iron screw coaster of 99 tons, she was built in 1823 and sold to Sir James Brooke, the hereditary Sultan of Sarawak, in 1859. After conversion, her tonnage was increased to 145.

Rajah An iron screw barque built in 1853. 537 gross tons. Transporting in Crimean War and then used as a bakery for the troops. In the late 1850's she was on the China Service. Sold in 1860.

Ripon A paddle barque with two funnels, built in 1846 of 1,508 gross tons. Transport in Crimean War. She was twice lengthened and in 1870 was given to Caird & Co. in part payment for *Pekin* and *Peshawur,* then converted into a sailing brig. A hulk at Trinidad in 1880 and later scuttled at sea. One claim to fame; in 1864 she carried Garibaldi to Britain.

Rowena* A Black Ball Line clipper, details unknown.

Royal Charter* Built in 1855 for a Liverpool firm who sold her while still under construction to Gibbs, Bright & Co. (Eagle Line). 2,719 gross tons. Three tall clipper masts with one funnel. See notes.

Salsette An iron screw, three-masted schooner, built in 1858 of 1,491 gross tons, later renamed *Sumatra.* Given new engines in 1873 and new boilers in 1890. Sold in 1898 and broken up in 1900.

Sarah Sands* The *Sarah Sands* was a vessel which caught fire in the 1850's while carrying troops from Cape Town to India. The damage sustained caused the vessel to drop anchor in Port Louis harbour where repairs were undertaken.

Shanghai An iron screw barque of 546 gross tons built in 1851. Chartered by the French Government in 1860/1 in Eastern troubles and finally sold in 1862.

Simla An iron screw steamer with three masts and one funnel, of 2,441 gross tons, built in 1854. Transporting during Crimean War. In 1860 her shaft broke when off Aden and she was towed in by *Candia* but was laid up for some time. In 1875 she was given to Howdens of Glasgow in part payment for the new compound engines of *Tanjore.* Foundered at sea after a collision in 1884.

Simoon* Details unknown.

Singapore Built in 1850 as sister ship to the *Ganges.* 1,190 gross tons, an iron paddle barque. 12 knots. In 1867 she struck a rock (afterwards known as Singapore Rock) while diverted from Yokohama to Hakodate to collect silkworm eggs. All hands were saved and the ship went down with all her flags flying.

Sir Jamsetjee Jeejeebhoy Built in 1855, a wooden paddle steamer of 125 gross tons employed at the Hong Kong station. Sold in 1856 to the Government to assist in the erection of a lighthouse off the south-eastern point of the Island of Ceylon.

Sydenham* Built in 1855, she was owned by Wilsons. 1,147 tons.

Teviot* A mail steamer owned by the East India Mail Company. The first gold to reach England from the diggings in Australia were shipped to Pernambucco in 1851 and then placed aboard the faster *Teviot.*

Thule* Arthur Anderson's own private yacht. Sold and presented to the Sultan of

Zanzibar. Thule was the old Latin name for Shetland, the birthplace of Anderson.

Trecinsor Details unknown.

Valetta Built in 1853, an iron paddler of 832 gross tons. 14 knots. Not successful at first as her engines were far too powerful but, when they were taken out and put into the much larger *Delta* and replaced by new engines by Penn, she was much better. Sold to the Egyptian Government in 1865.

Vectis The second P&O ship of this name. A paddle steamer and the first ship to use the improved diagonal system of wooden planking. Built in 1853. Barquentine with two funnels. The original engine proved to be too powerful and was later taken out and put into the *Massilia* in 1863. 841 gross tons. Sold to the Egyptians in 1865.

Victoria* *HMAS Victoria*, a screw corvette.

Victoria* Kendall travelled by the new packet *Victoria* introduced on the Folkestone to Boulogne run by the South Eastern Railway.

West* Probably, a "fast sailing barque" of 409 tons operated by Thornton & Wests between London and Singapore.

Wonga Wonga* An Australian clipper steamer, details unknown.

Wyoming* A wooden screw sloop of war of 997 tons, barque-rigged with 7 guns. Launched on the Delaware in January 1859. Based on the Asiatic Station until 1867 and then operated in the Atlantic and Mediterranean until decommissioned in 1882. Searched for Confederate shipping in 1863 off Singapore.

10 Wreck of the *Alma* in the Red Sea in 1859.

170

Index

172